SELF-CARE(ISH) SANITY HACKS

A Humorous Guide to Surviving the Chaos of Everyday Life

AVERY WELLS

Contents

Introduction

Self-care has become quite the buzzword, hasn't it? Just scroll through social media, and it's all face masks, luxurious baths, and perfectly curated "me time" that looks suspiciously like a magazine ad. Every influencer seems to have hours to spare lounging in silk robes, sipping herbal tea, and meditating in front of a scenic window. But let's be real: most of us don't have the time, energy, or perfectly styled hair to live that life. For those of us trying to juggle work, family, errands, and maybe squeezing in a hobby if we're lucky, self-care often sounds like one more thing to do, or worse—an impossible ideal that only people with a personal assistant and a yoga guru can pull off.

But here's the thing: self-care doesn't have to mean rearranging your schedule or relocating to a wellness retreat in the mountains. You don't need an entire day off, a complicated spa regimen, or even a Pinterest-worthy planner to care for yourself. Self-care is about the small things, the quick wins, and finding moments of calm amidst the chaos. It's about taking a breath when you feel like screaming or turning that mindless chore into a moment of peace. With just a few simple shifts, you can turn your everyday chaos into tiny opportunities for self-care—even if your life feels more like a never-ending to-do list than an influencer's highlight reel.

This book is for people who roll their eyes at the idea of dedicating two hours to journaling or meticulously diffusing essential oils. It's for the parents who can't use the bathroom without an audience, the professionals glued to their email 24/7, and anyone who's ever thought, "Who has time for self-care when I'm just trying to survive the day?" Self-care doesn't have to be pretty, perfect, or Instagram-worthy—it just has to work for you.

If your idea of a morning ritual is hitting snooze three times and hoping there's still coffee in the cupboard, you're in the right place. We're going to redefine self-care, stripping away the fluff and making it accessible, doable, and, best of all, realistic. Think of this book as your guide to messy, chaotic, beautifully imperfect self-care. We'll laugh at the fails, embrace the small victories, and find ways to carve out moments of calm—even if it's just deep breathing while you brush your teeth.

By the end of this book, you'll know how to sneak self-care into even the busiest days. You'll learn to find peace in the middle of the morning rush, turn chores into moments of mindfulness, and maybe even reclaim a sliver of your sanity. And you won't need a yoga mat, a retreat center, or an army of babysitters to do it. Sound good? Let's dive in, starting with the chaos of the morning rush, and see how surprisingly easy self-care can be when it's tailored to real life.

ONE

Morning Survival Techniques (A.K.A. Self-Care on Fast-Forward)

Mornings are supposed to be peaceful and quiet, right? They often feel like a sprint with extra caffeine, except in real life. Between hunting for keys, spilling coffee, and trying to remember if you let the dog out, there's barely a moment to breathe, let alone meditate. But what if you could sneak some self-care into your morning without adding more to your plate? This chapter is about just that—simple techniques to make mornings feel a little less like chaos and a little more like...something you can actually look forward to.

Quick Morning Mindfulness: Setting the Tone for the Day

Most mornings, it's a miracle if we even get out of bed, let alone start the day with calm intentions. But here's a secret: you don't need a perfect morning routine to set yourself up for a better day. Even in the first groggy minutes after you wake up, just a few tiny adjustments can make a surprising difference.

Start with the easiest win: take a few deep breaths before you grab your phone. I know that phone calls you with notifications and maybe a few memes you're dying to see, but hold off for just a second. Instead, take three deep breaths, feel the weight of the blankets, and take in the quiet—before the day's to-do list tries to storm your brain. This tiny pause is like a gentle alarm for your mind, a way to ease into the day without diving straight into the chaos.

While you're waiting for the coffee to brew, try a quick "gratitude" moment. And no, you don't have to come up with something deep. Just think of one little thing you're grateful for: the coffee itself, the way the sunlight hits the window, or the dog didn't wake you up at 4 a.m. (for once). Taking even 15 seconds to notice something good in the morning is a small but powerful way to boost yourself mentally. You'll be surprised how far this tiny practice can go in helping you feel grounded and calm, even if only until your first meeting.

And remember, self-care doesn't have to mean adding anything extra to your routine. While you're brushing your teeth, try taking slow, deep breaths—each one a reminder to start the day on a calmer note. If you're feeling adventurous, turn moisturizing into a mini-moment of mindfulness. Yep, even rubbing lotion on your hands can be a self-care practice. Focus on the feeling of your hands, the smell of the lotion, or just the fact that you're taking a second to care for yourself. These small moments of mindfulness don't take any extra time, but they're sneaky little pauses of calm that turn the usual morning rush into something that feels...almost pleasant.

If you can swing it, try adding just five minutes for a mini morning ritual. I know, five minutes is asking a lot in the morning, but hear me out. A quick stretch, a deep breath, or setting a simple intention like "stay sane" can work wonders. Just those few minutes to focus on yourself can make you feel like you've got a handle on things before the day tries to take control.

Even the busiest mornings can feel more manageable with these tiny shifts. Self-care isn't about perfection; it's about finding those moments of calm in the middle of real life. And if you can start the day with a few deep breaths, a gratitude check, and maybe a little lotion mindfulness, you're already winning at the self-care game.

The "Between Tasks" Self-Care Method

Let's be real: life sometimes feels like an endless parade of tasks. It's like a relay race, except the finish line keeps moving, and instead of a prize at the end, you're rewarded with more emails, errands, and maybe a reminder to "schedule self-care," which feels ironic at best. But here's the twist: you don't actually need a long, dedicated break to recharge. With a little creativity, those fleeting seconds between tasks can turn into tiny mental vacations—no passport or paid time off required.

Think about those small gaps in your day that usually feel like time fillers. Waiting in line? Stuck in traffic? Standing by the coffee maker as it brews your fuel for the day? These "micro-moments" are prime time for sneaky self-care moves. Instead of scrolling through your phone or staring at the microwave, try using these seconds to do something refreshingly simple: breathe. Yes, breathe—intentionally, deeply, slowly. The kind of breathing that signals your brain to relax, even if you're just standing in the printer line or fidgeting in your car. Taking three slow breaths is like a mini vacation for your mind, tricking it into thinking it's taking a break, even if reality says otherwise.

If breathing exercises don't quite do it for you, you can tap into the power of imagination. Picture this: as you're standing there, close your eyes (or keep them open if you don't want coworkers thinking you've decided to nap standing up) and visualize your "happy place." For some, this might be a beach with waves rolling in; for others, it's a cabin in the woods, or maybe just your couch with zero responsibilities in sight. Visualize the sounds, smells, and overall feeling of calm in that place. Visualization is like a budget-friendly vacation—short, effective, and doesn't require you to pack sunscreen. Just a few seconds of this mental getaway can make all the difference in approaching the next task on your list.

Another quick trick is the "body check-in." This might sound fancy, but all it involves is noticing if you're sitting like a pretzel and, well, un-pretzeling yourself. Are your shoulders tense? Is your jaw clenched? If you're using your shoulders as earrings, it's time to let them drop. A quick body check reminds you to relax and helps avoid the build-up of stress that seems to creep into the muscles throughout the day. You don't need to go into a full yoga stretch; sometimes, just rolling your shoulders or straightening your posture is enough to give your body a break and feel a bit more human and a bit less like a crumpled piece of paper.

Of course, turning these in-between moments into self-care doesn't mean hitting "pause" on life or holding up traffic to meditate in the middle of the crosswalk. These are mini pauses that add refreshment without any noticeable disruption. In just a few seconds, you're giving yourself a mental reset, a small yet effective way to calm the mind and body. It's a subtle change that can transform a day, helping you avoid that all-too-familiar feeling of being completely fried by 3 p.m.

So, the next time you find yourself waiting for a website to load, a coffee to brew, or a line to move, give one of these micro-moves a try. These small, mindful moments add up, leaving you a bit less frazzled and a bit more grounded by the end of the day. Who knew self-care could be this sneaky, this simple, and maybe even this satisfying? Embracing these in-between moments is like finding little pockets of calm hiding throughout your day. By the time the day wraps up, you'll have built up a series of refreshers—one tiny, sneaky self-care moment at a time.

Self-Care at Work: Staying Sane at Your Desk

Ah, the office—a place filled with fluorescent lighting, endless emails, and the delicate sound of keyboards clicking away. Whether you're working from home or back at the office, workdays have a way of piling on the stress. But believe it or not, you can squeeze in self-care at your desk without attracting too much attention or looking like you're trying to stage a mini yoga retreat. With just a few sneaky moves, you can create a bit of calm right in the middle of the workday chaos.

Let's start with the easiest trick in the book: a quick stretch. Desk stretches don't have to be dramatic. You don't need to fling your arms around like you're in a dance class, but a subtle shoulder roll or two? Perfect. Just shrug those shoulders up to your ears, take a deep breath, and let them drop. It's like telling your body, "Hey, no need to hold onto all that tension." You'll look casual and feel a little looser, and no one has to know you're secretly practicing self-care right there in the middle of your inbox marathon.

Next, consider turning your computer screen into a "calm zone." I know that's a stretch but stay with me here. Pick a calming desktop wallpaper, something like a serene beach or a quiet mountain lake—basically, anything that doesn't scream "productivity." Every time you minimize a window, it's like a two-second visual break, a reminder that there's a world beyond spreadsheets and emails. And if anyone asks, you can just say, "It helps me focus." Not exactly true, but close enough.

Then there's the trusty "desk stretch under the desk" move, also known as the toe point or foot roll. This is for the days when sitting still turns your legs to stone. Point your toes, flex your feet, or circle your ankles a few times under the desk without getting up. Not only does this improve circulation (no one likes tingly feet), but it also gives you a sense of sneaky satisfaction—you're technically exercising while answering emails.

Another easy self-care trick? Hydrate. I know water sounds boring compared to coffee, but it does wonders for keeping you refreshed. Get a water bottle you actually like (bonus points if it has motivational quotes or a built-in straw) and keep it within reach. Take a sip every time you finish an email or complete a task, and voila! You're hydrating and creating mini-breaks. Plus, those trips to refill your water bottle give you a reason to stand up and walk around, which counts as a mini break without looking like you're taking one.

If you're feeling bold, try desk yoga—but make it subtle. We're not talking about a full tree pose in the middle of the office; instead, try a seated twist. Just put one hand on the back of your chair, gently twist, and take a breath. It's an inconspicuous and effective move, giving your spine a nice stretch while helping you feel a bit more centered. It's like a secret recharge button for your body.

And finally, let's not forget the power of the occasional deep breath. Think of it as your in-office reset button. When you're feeling overwhelmed by a never-ending to-do list, just close your eyes (if you're in a safe spot to do so), take a long breath in, and let it out slowly. You'd be surprised how much one deep breath can slow things down, even if just for a moment. It's simple and effective, and no one's the wiser.

With these subtle techniques, you're transforming your desk into a tiny oasis where self-care can thrive amid work demands. No one else needs to know that your shoulder shrugs, foot flexes, or deep breaths are part of a secret self-care regimen. By weaving these little moments into your day, you're keeping stress levels in check without missing a single email. And by the time the workday ends, you'll feel a little less frazzled and a little more refreshed—desk yoga and all.

Turning Daily Chores into Moments of Calm

Chores—whether it's laundry, dishes, or vacuuming—seem to have a knack for sneaking into our schedules when we'd rather be doing anything else. But here's the surprising twist: these necessary tasks don't have to feel like a drain on your energy. With a small shift in mindset, even the most mundane chores can double as self-care, offering tiny pockets of calm and mindfulness. Yes, you read that right. Chores can actually help you unwind.

Let's start with dishwashing. It's a famously repetitive task that often makes us wish we had a live-in dishwasher. But next time you're faced with a sink full of dishes, try slowing down and making it a mini-meditation. Feel the warmth of the water, notice the bubbles, and appreciate the rhythmic motion of scrubbing. Instead of rushing through, give each dish a little extra attention—as if even the coffee cup you've refilled a dozen times today deserves its moment in the spotlight. By focusing on the sensations and keeping your mind present, you're transforming dishwashing into a surprisingly peaceful activity. Who would've thought scrubbing pots could bring a sense of calm?

Then there's laundry. Folding clothes may not sound exciting, but with a mindful approach, it can be almost...calming. Set yourself up with a comfortable spot, a good playlist, or a podcast you enjoy, and begin folding slowly. Feel the textures of each item, smooth out the wrinkles, and take your time. Each fold is like a small act of self-care, bringing a sense of order to your day one sock at a time. It's a quiet little victory, transforming that mountain of clothes into neatly stacked piles. You're not just folding laundry—you're creating a bit of calm.

Sweeping or vacuuming might sound too noisy to be relaxing, but it's a surprisingly satisfying chore once you get into the rhythm. Imagine each sweep or push of the vacuum as "clearing away" stress.

With each motion, let go of a little tension. Focus on the movement, the sounds, and the small satisfaction of seeing crumbs disappear. It's like clearing your mind as you clean the floor. And the best part? You get an instant, tangible result: a tidy space and a lighter mood.

If you're ready for a little adventure in mindfulness, try organizing a drawer. We all have that one drawer—the "junk drawer" where everything lands when it has nowhere else to go. Instead of dreading it, turn it into a mini-project. As you sort through random pens, spare keys, and that mysterious charger that seems to belong to nothing, you're not just organizing physical space but giving your mind a small break. There's something soothing about putting things in order, even if it's just one drawer. And the sense of accomplishment when you're done? It's an added bonus of self-care.

Of course, none of this is to say that you need to love chores. It's more about finding those small, mindful moments that turn necessary tasks into tiny mental breaks. Imagine each chore as a chance to unwind without even leaving the house. You're multitasking in the best possible way—cleaning up your space and refreshing your mind.

So, the next time you're faced with a pile of dishes, a mountain of laundry, or a vacuum, try shifting your approach. Slow down, pay attention to the details, and treat each chore like a little act of care for both yourself and your space. You're turning your to-do list into a "to-relax" list by transforming mundane tasks into mindful moments. You'll finish with a cleaner home, a clearer mind, and maybe—just maybe—a newfound appreciation for chores. Well, at least until they pile up again tomorrow.

As we've seen, self-care doesn't require grand gestures or perfectly curated routines. Even in the middle of chaotic mornings or mundane chores, there are opportunities to build in small moments of mindfulness and calm. By simply shifting how you approach each task—whether it's dishwashing or starting the day with a deep breath

—you're creating pockets of peace that add up over time. Now that we've covered mornings and those little pockets of calm within daily tasks, it's time to look at the spaces in between. In the next chapter, we'll dive into self-care techniques you can use in the "in-between" moments—those quick breaks, commutes, and waiting times that we often overlook but can turn into some of the best times to recharge.

TWO

The "Between Things" Self-Care Method

Life has a funny way of filling itself with awkward pauses—the waiting room stints, the lines at the grocery store, the eternal hold music on customer service calls. These little in-between moments are scattered all over the day, like cosmic reminders that we're not as busy as we think. But here's the twist: instead of using these moments to scroll through your phone or plan a daring escape from adulthood, what if you turned them into quick self-care breaks? In this chapter, we'll explore how to make the most of these waiting gaps. No need for a day off or a meditation retreat; sometimes, all you need is a few seconds between tasks to catch your breath, recharge, and maybe even trick yourself into feeling like you're on a mini-vacation.

Using Moments Between Tasks (Like Commuting or Waiting) as Micro-Breaks

If life's little in-between moments—waiting rooms, red lights, the awkward three minutes while your coffee reheats—are starting to feel like lost time, it's time for a reframe. These tiny gaps aren't just empty spaces; they're micro-breaks hiding in plain sight. With a little creativity, you can use them as sneaky self-care intervals, turning minutes that might otherwise feel wasted into a mini reset for your mind.

Think about it: instead of fidgeting while the doctor's office is running 15 minutes late (which it always is), try a quick breathing exercise. This doesn't have to be a grand production. Take three deep breaths, counting to four on each inhale and exhale. No one needs to know you're "meditating." For all they know, you're just really into breathing—which, technically, you are. Those three breaths can work wonders for dialing down stress and helping you feel a little more Zen before the next appointment, grocery run, or whatever else awaits.

And speaking of grocery lines, that's prime real estate for self-care, believe it or not. Instead of debating if you should have gone to the other line (the one that's now moving faster), focus on something simple and grounding. You could do a quick mental check-in, asking yourself how you're feeling in that moment, or just notice the sounds around you—the beeping scanners, murmured conversations, maybe a toddler nearby wondering why they can't have candy. Staying present, even in line, turns the wait into a small chance to reset.

Commutes, especially, are fertile ground for sneaky self-care. If you're driving, try a little visualization exercise at every red light. Picture yourself in a place you love—a beach, a mountain cabin, or even a silent, people-free zone that feels like a dream escape. Imagine the sights, smells, and feelings of that place, letting it wash over you for just a moment before the light turns green. It's like a mental vacation that takes all of 30 seconds but leaves you feeling surprisingly refreshed. Just, you know, keep one eye on the road while you're in your mental paradise.

If you're on public transit, your options open up even more. Put on a favorite podcast, listen to a soothing playlist, or even try a simple meditation app. No one's going to interrupt you (if they're following commuter etiquette, that is), so you have permission to zone out and use that time to unwind. You're not just getting from Point A to Point B—you're taking a little breather before the day throws something new at you.

Another quick way to transform these in-between moments is with a mental gratitude check. Now, I get it; gratitude checks can sound like something that requires a big production, but it's as simple as thinking of one or two things you're thankful for. It could be anything—your morning coffee, the fact that you didn't miss the bus, or that you remembered to bring snacks. Just acknowledging a small, positive thing can make you feel more grounded, no candles or journal required.

Lastly, let's talk about those few minutes while your computer restarts, which usually involves pacing the floor or staring blankly at the loading screen. Instead, use that brief lull to stand up, stretch, and maybe even roll your shoulders or do a quick neck stretch. It's like a mini-reset for your body and mind, all while you're waiting for your tech to cooperate. Plus, if anyone asks, you can say you're "in a wellness routine"—which is exactly true.

These micro-breaks don't need to be elaborate or lengthy to be effective. Just a few intentional breaths, a gratitude thought, or a visualization at a red light can transform those waiting periods into opportunities for refreshment. Instead of letting these moments pass unnoticed, use them to recharge in a way that leaves you feeling less frazzled and more prepared for whatever comes next. Life may be busy, but with a few sneaky self-care moves, even the smallest gaps in your day can become chances to reset and recharge.

Five-Minute Breathing Techniques for Public Places

Navigating public places can sometimes feel like an exercise in patience. Whether you're waiting in line, commuting, or sitting in a crowded room, stress can creep up quickly. The good news? With just a few subtle breathing techniques, you can create your own little bubble of calm—no yoga mat required. These techniques are quiet and effective, and no one even has to know you're doing them.

Let's start with a classic: *The 4-4-4 Breath.* This technique is simple and perfect for times when you need a mental breather without looking like you're about to faint. Inhale slowly for four seconds, hold it for another four seconds, then exhale for four seconds. Repeat a few times, and you'll start feeling a sense of calm as if you're resetting your inner system. It's great for those moments when you're stuck in a line that isn't moving, surrounded by strangers who all look just as tired as you. It's also subtle enough that no one will wonder what you're doing—except maybe why you're the only one who looks relaxed.

Another favorite is *The Sigh of Relief.* Okay, so sighing isn't exactly groundbreaking, but it works wonders. Take a deep breath in and then exhale with a soft sigh. This can be done quietly, so it doesn't seem like you're sighing over life's disappointments (even if you are). The exhale tells your body to relax, signaling that the coast is clear—even if "the coast" is a line of people at the coffee shop. You'd be surprised how something as simple as a sigh can release tension and bring a sense of ease.

Box Breathing is another subtle trick that's great for calming down when things feel a bit too hectic. Picture a box in your mind. Inhale for four counts, hold for four, exhale for four, and hold again for four. Repeat this cycle as you visualize each "side" of the box. This little exercise not only helps you calm down but gives your mind something simple to focus on besides the long wait or the person who's talking loudly on their phone right next to you.

If you want to go even simpler, try *Counting Down Breaths*. This one is perfect for passing the time or calming down before a stressful appointment. Start by taking a deep breath, and as you exhale, mentally count "five." With the next exhale, count "four," and so on down to "one." When you reach one, start again. It's an easy, no-frills way to keep your mind focused, and it's pretty much guaranteed that no one will have a clue you're doing it. It's like your own personal, invisible "calm-down countdown."

One of the most powerful but least flashy techniques is *The 5-Second Exhale—this* one's ideal for moments when you're feeling extra stressed. Breathe in naturally, then exhale slowly for five full seconds. The long exhale taps into your body's natural relaxation response, which helps you unwind even if you're on a noisy subway or in a crowded café. Just repeat a few times, and you'll feel the difference. The extended exhale works almost like a mental "off switch" for stress, quieting your mind even if everything around you is chaotic.

These quick breathing exercises are like little "emergency exits" for your mind, offering calm wherever you are. They're the perfect tools for reclaiming a sense of peace in public places, whether you're in a line, on a train, or just stuck in a crowded room. Best of all, these techniques are so subtle and simple that you can use them anytime without drawing attention.

So, next time you're in a stressful public setting, try one of these techniques. In just five minutes, you can create a mini oasis of calm, making it through the day with less stress and much more ease.

Visualization Hacks for Everyday Situations

Sometimes, you just need to escape—even if you're standing in a grocery store line or waiting for a meeting to start. Visualization is like a mental teleportation device: you can be on a beach or in the mountains without anyone knowing you're miles away in your mind. These visualization hacks are subtle, powerful, and perfect for creating a mental vacation amid everyday chaos.

Let's start with the *Classic Beach Scene.* This one's popular because it's easy to picture, even if your last beach vacation was years ago. Imagine the feel of warm sand underfoot, the sound of waves rolling in, and the distant call of seagulls. You can even throw in the scent of sunscreen if you want the full effect. The trick is to focus on the sensory details. Feel the sun on your skin, hear the waves, and let your mind sink into this imaginary beach for a few moments. This visualization is ideal for those moments when you're in a loud or crowded place—it's like an instant mental getaway that leaves you feeling calmer and maybe even a little sun-kissed.

Try creating your own Happy Place if the beach isn't your thing. This could be a quiet forest, a cozy cabin, or even your childhood backyard. Pick a place that feels comforting and personal, then visualize yourself there. Picture the details—the colors, the smells, the sounds. Maybe you're hearing birds in the trees, feeling a gentle breeze, or even noticing the smell of pine. Creating your own mental sanctuary allows you to escape stress and return to a place that feels like home, even if it's only in your mind. This is especially handy for moments when you're feeling overwhelmed and need a quick mental reset.

For a more active visualization, there's *The Forest Walk.* Picture yourself strolling through a peaceful forest surrounded by tall trees and dappled sunlight. With each "step," imagine the feeling of soft earth under your feet, the rustle of leaves, and the cool, fresh air. Take a mental pause to listen to birds or the distant sound of a stream. The best part? You don't need to actually walk anywhere, so this one works even if you're just waiting at a bus stop. This forest walk can make you feel grounded and relaxed, like a short, refreshing hike for the mind.

If floating sounds more relaxing, try *The Lake Float*. Imagine yourself lying on a calm lake, completely weightless. You're on your back, the water is supporting you, and there's a gentle sun warming your face. Feel yourself float, watching clouds drift by above, and imagine any stress just floating away with the ripples in the water. This visualization is great for moments when you're feeling really tense and need a soothing escape. Just a minute or two of "floating" can calm your mind and make you feel like you've just left a spa (without the hefty bill).

One last visualization that's easy to slip into anywhere is *The Cloud Watching*. Imagine yourself lying in an open field, looking up at a sky full of drifting clouds. Let your mind follow each cloud as it floats by, observing the different shapes and sizes. This exercise is especially helpful when you're feeling anxious or restless. Watching the clouds in your mind is like pressing "pause" on your worries, giving you a mental break that lets you slow down.

These visualizations don't require any special skills or even much time. Just pick a scene that resonates with you, focus on the details, and let yourself "go there" for a few moments. Each one of these mental escapes can help you recharge and find a sense of calm no matter where you are.

So, the next time you need a mini-vacation, try one of these visualizations. Just a minute or two can bring you back to reality, feeling more grounded and less frazzled, even if you never left the grocery store line.

How to Recharge with Mini-Breaks Between Busy Tasks

Life often feels like a nonstop relay race where each task hands you off to the next. By the time you finish one thing, you're already thinking about the next five. But what if you used those tiny moments between tasks—waiting for a file to download, standing in line, or even microwaving your lunch—as opportunities for a quick recharge? These mini-breaks don't require much time or space and can give you just enough of a reset to keep you going strong.

Start with something as simple as an *"Eye Break."* If you've been staring at a screen all day, your eyes are probably feeling the strain. Next time you're waiting for an email to send or a file to load, look away from your screen and focus on something 20 feet away. Find a window, a plant across the room, or even the inspirational poster someone put up on the office wall. Give your eyes a chance to "stretch" for just a few seconds. It's like a tiny workout for your vision—no squinting required.

Another favorite is the *"Mindful Sip."* Grab your water bottle, coffee, or tea, and instead of taking a quick gulp, take a slow, intentional sip. Focus on the taste, the warmth or coolness, and the sensation of swallowing. It sounds almost too simple, but this tiny pause can be surprisingly refreshing. Plus, staying hydrated has the added benefit of keeping you alert—just one more reason to make this a regular mini-break throughout your day.

The *"Invisible Leg Stretch"* can be a lifesaver when you feel stiff. Without even getting out of your chair, straighten one leg under the desk, flex your foot, and hold it for a few seconds. Alternate with the other leg, or do a few reps if you're feeling ambitious. It's subtle, so you won't look like you're secretly doing a workout in the middle of the office. But your legs will thank you later, especially if you've been sitting for hours.

Then there's the *"5-Second Reset."* This one's so fast and easy you'll wonder why you haven't been doing it all along. Close your eyes (unless you're in a public place where closing your eyes could be risky), take a deep breath, and let it out slowly. Imagine that you're letting go of a little stress with each exhale. Just five seconds is all it takes, but it's like a mental refresh button. You'll feel calmer, more focused, and ready to dive into the next task.

Another great option for these mini-breaks is the *"Counting Breath."* Next time you have a moment, take a few deep breaths and count each exhale. Try to get to five, then start over. The counting adds a layer of focus, helping to keep any wandering thoughts at bay. This mini-break works wonders for high-stress moments, like before a big presentation or during a hectic day. It's like grounding yourself without anyone even noticing.

And let's not forget the power of a good stretch for your neck and shoulders. Just roll your shoulders back a few times, stretch your neck from side to side, or do a quick shoulder shrug. These small movements help relieve tension from hours spent hunched over a screen or stuck in a chair. It's like telling your body, "Hey, I haven't forgotten about you!"

Using these mini-breaks between tasks keeps stress in check and gives your body and mind the tiny refreshers they need. None of these take more than a few seconds, but they can make a huge difference in how you feel by the end of the day. Instead of feeling drained, you'll be able to tackle each task with a little more energy and a lot less tension.

Next time you're about to jump into your next to-do, try one of these tiny resets. They might just turn that long, endless relay of tasks into a series of manageable, refreshing pauses.

By turning those small, in-between moments into mini self-care breaks, you're unlocking a secret weapon for staying refreshed, even on the busiest days. From quick breathing exercises to visualizing a peaceful escape, these tiny practices help you reset, recharge, and stay grounded. The best part? They fit seamlessly into your day without adding anything extra to your schedule. But what about when you're at work, tethered to your desk and drowning in emails? In the next chapter, we'll explore self-care techniques you can practice right at your desk, helping you stay calm and focused without drawing too much attention—or looking like you're trying to meditate in the middle of a meeting.

THREE

Self-Care at Work—Staying Sane at Your Desk

The workday has its own unique kind of chaos: back-to-back emails, surprise meetings, and the slow but steady tension that builds after hours at a desk. But self-care at work doesn't have to mean slipping away for a meditation session or putting a "Do Not Disturb" sign on your office door. In this chapter, we'll explore practical self-care tips to help you stay sane and grounded at your desk. With just a few sneaky moves, you can create a sense of calm and clarity, even if your inbox is overflowing.

Desk Stretches and Movements That Won't Draw Attention

Let's be honest: sitting at a desk for hours can turn you into a human pretzel. Shoulders are tense, neck aching, and legs feel like they've morphed into concrete. Does that sound familiar? But the idea of full-on stretches in the middle of the office might feel a bit awkward (not to mention it's hard to focus when everyone's watching you attempt a yoga pose in work clothes). Fortunately, there are subtle ways to stretch at your desk that will help relieve tension without raising eyebrows.

First up: the *Shoulder Shrug*. This move is so subtle that people might just think you're pondering something deep or mulling over the latest email. All you have to do is lift your shoulders up toward your ears, hold for a few seconds, and then let them drop. Repeat a few times, and you'll feel the tension start to melt away. It's like telling your body, "Hey, we're not actually carrying the weight of the world—just pretending to." Bonus points if you add a deep breath with each shrug.

Next, we have the *Seated Twist*. Sitting up tall, place your right hand on the back of your chair and gently twist your torso to the right, using the chair as leverage. Hold for a couple of breaths, then repeat on the other side. This is great for releasing tension in the back, and it looks subtle enough that no one will assume you're practicing for a yoga class. It's just a little move that keeps your spine happy and makes sitting for hours slightly more bearable.

For the legs, try the *Invisible Leg Stretch*. This one's perfect because you don't even have to leave your chair. Extend one leg out in front of you, flex your foot, and hold for a few seconds before pointing your toes and holding again. Alternate between flexing and pointing, then switch to the other leg. This keeps your leg muscles from stiffening up and promotes circulation—no need for anyone to know you're working on your flexibility while answering emails.

If your calves are feeling tight, the *Under-the-Desk Calf Raise* is a game-changer. Keep both feet flat on the floor, then lift your heels so only your toes are touching the ground. Lower back down and repeat a few times. You're giving your calves a mini workout without standing up, and it's subtle enough that no one will even notice. It's perfect for those days when you're in back-to-back meetings and can't step away from your desk.

And don't forget the *Neck Roll*. When the stress of staring at screens has your neck feeling like it's locked in place, try this simple move. Drop your chin toward your chest, then slowly roll your neck from one shoulder to the other. Do this a couple of times to release any tension, being mindful of any tight spots along the way. Not only will you feel a wave of relief, but you'll also look like you're thoughtfully processing information—very professional.

The best part about these desk stretches? They're quick, effective, and low-profile, allowing you to work a little self-care into the day without making it a big production. You're not only keeping your muscles loose but also giving your mind a mini-break from the constant demands of work.

So, next time you're feeling like a bundle of tension by noon, try one of these stealthy moves. In just a few seconds, you'll be feeling a bit more relaxed and ready to tackle whatever comes next in the workday marathon. These stretches are your secret weapon for staying sanc and comfortable at your desk—no dramatic poses required.

Digital Detox Tips for Screen-Heavy Workdays

If you're spending hours glued to a screen, you're not alone. Screen time can sneak up on us fast between emails, virtual meetings, and the occasional (okay, frequent) doom-scrolling session. The problem? Too much screen time can leave you feeling drained, foggy, and ready to throw your laptop out the window. But you don't need to pull the plug entirely to feel a little more refreshed. With some sneaky digital detox tricks, you can keep the screen fatigue at bay without falling behind on your work.

First up: *The 20-20-20 Rule.* It's the easiest, least intrusive digital detox hack out there. Every 20 minutes, look at something 20 feet away for at least 20 seconds. This gives your eyes a much-needed break from staring at the screen, helping reduce eye strain and the all-too-familiar "screen squint." You can set a quiet timer on your computer or phone to remind you to glance away. If anyone catches you staring out the window, you can say you're "refreshing your vision." Sounds legitimate, right?

Another tip? *Designate "No-Screen" Zones.* Think of it like setting boundaries—but for your screens. Pick a spot in your workspace or home where screens are off-limits. Maybe it's a cozy chair where you can read a real book (yes, they still exist), a lunch table where you can eat without scrolling, or even a section of your desk where you keep a plant instead of your phone. Creating these no-screen zones gives your brain a mini digital vacation whenever you enter that space.

Then there's *Do Not Disturb Mode.* This feature isn't just for avoiding late-night texts; it's a fantastic tool to help you focus during work hours. By setting your phone to "Do Not Disturb," you avoid the temptation of every notification, ping, and buzz. No more checking your phone every two minutes—now, it's just you and the task at hand. Your phone will be waiting with all its notifications, but only when you're ready. Consider it a modern twist on "out of sight, out of mind."

To give your eyes a break, try *Blue Light Blocking.* Many devices have built-in settings that reduce blue light, especially in the evening. Blue light, if you're wondering, is the culprit behind those late-night headaches and trouble falling asleep. You can also snag a pair of blue-light-blocking glasses if you want the full effect. Either way, you're doing your eyes a favor by toning down that blue hue, especially if you're burning the midnight oil.

If you're itching to scroll or click something mindless, try a *Micro-Meditation Break.* These can be as quick as 30 seconds and help clear your mind without needing to pick up your phone. Close your eyes, take a few deep breaths, and visualize something calming —like a beach, a forest, or maybe even a place with zero Wi-Fi. These tiny meditations give your brain a mini-break from the digital onslaught, letting you refocus without needing a lengthy retreat.

Another trick that's weirdly satisfying? *Desktop Decluttering.* Clutter doesn't just apply to your physical space; it can also be a problem on your computer. Take a few minutes to clear out old files, organize your desktop, and close any open tabs that aren't essential. This "digital cleanup" is like a breath of fresh air for your brain. You'll feel more focused and less overwhelmed, especially if your desktop looks like a file graveyard.

Digital detoxing isn't about going offline entirely; it's about giving yourself tiny, refreshing breaks from screen time so you don't hit burnout by noon. These tips let you step back from the digital world without totally disconnecting, allowing you to feel more focused, alert, and ready to tackle the next task.

So, try one of these detox tips next time you're feeling screen fatigue creeping up. You can stay digitally connected without feeling drained with just a few adjustments. You'll thank yourself—and so will your tired eyes.

Quick Breathing Exercises to Handle Work Stress on the Spot

Work stress has a way of sneaking up on you. One minute, you're cruising through emails; the next, you're in the middle of a three-hour meeting that could've been an email. The good news? You don't need a spa day to find some calm. A few quick breathing exercises can help you manage stress on the spot, bringing a little peace to even the busiest workdays. And the best part? These techniques are subtle, so you won't look like you're trying to perform an interpretive dance at your desk.

First up is *The 4-4-4 Breath.* It's as simple as it sounds. Inhale slowly for four seconds, hold your breath for another four seconds and then exhale for four seconds. Repeat this a few times, and you'll feel slightly calmer as if you just pressed "refresh" on your mind. It's perfect for those moments when you're trying to decipher a confusing email or in a meeting that feels like it might never end. Just keep it subtle—no one needs to know you're practicing zen breathing; they'll just assume you're very calm.

Then there's the *Sigh of Relief.* This one's a bit louder, but it's surprisingly effective. Take a deep breath, and as you exhale, let out a soft sigh. Not a dramatic sigh (save that one for when you're home) —just a gentle release. The sighing sound is a signal to your nervous system to relax. It's perfect for those moments when you feel overwhelmed but don't want to look too obvious. If anyone asks, you can always say, "Just breathing my way to clarity!"

Box Breathing is another great technique for calming down during a hectic day. Picture a box in your mind: inhale as you visualize drawing the first side of the box for four counts, hold your breath for four counts as you draw the second side, exhale for four counts as you draw the third side, and hold for four counts as you complete the box. This structured breathing exercise is ideal for grounding yourself, especially if you feel scattered or anxious. Plus, it's quiet, so you can do it in an open office without anyone batting an eye.

If you're short on time or just need something quick, try the *5-Second Exhale.* Take a deep breath in, then exhale slowly for five full seconds. The long exhale taps into your body's relaxation response, instantly calming your nervous system. This is perfect for those moments when stress is about to hit "meltdown" level. It's like telling your brain, "Hey, we're not in crisis mode—calm down." Repeat a few times, and you'll feel the tension melt away.

For those who want to keep things extra simple, there's the *Counting Breath.* As you inhale and exhale, simply count each breath. Start by counting up to five, then start over. This repetitive counting is a sneaky way to keep your mind focused, making it perfect for moments when stress is high but you don't have the luxury of stepping away from your desk. This technique is especially helpful before tackling a big project or presentation, allowing you to anchor your mind in the moment.

Each exercise is a quick fix for stress, helping you pause and reset before diving back into work. You don't need a meditation app or fancy setup—just a few deep breaths can work wonders. The beauty of these techniques is their simplicity. You're taking a few seconds for yourself, which adds up over time, leaving you feeling a little more centered and much less stressed.

So next time work stress starts piling on, remember these quick breathing exercises. With just a few subtle breaths, you're reclaiming a bit of calm in your day, no matter what's going on around you. It's the kind of self-care that fits any schedule—no extra effort required.

Ideas for Transforming Your Workspace into a Calm Zone

When work stress builds up, your workspace can sometimes feel like anything but a calm, productive place. But what if you could make your desk or office a mini sanctuary? You don't need a total makeover to create a calm zone at work. Just a few small changes can make your workspace feel a little more like your own personal retreat—and a lot less like a stress zone.

Start with something simple: Bring in a Plant. Plants add a touch of nature to any workspace, instantly making things feel fresher and calmer. A small plant like a succulent or a snake plant is low-maintenance (they practically thrive on neglect), so you don't have to worry about becoming an amateur botanist. Just looking at something green can be surprisingly soothing, and as a bonus, plants also improve air quality. So really, it's like your plant is working right alongside you, offering a little dose of zen as you tackle your to-do list.

Next, consider creating a little "Reset Corner" on your desk. This could be a small space reserved for items that help you relax—a stress ball, a tiny jar of candy, a soothing stone, or even a photo that makes you smile. You can glance at or reach for your "reset" item whenever you feel stress creeping in. This mini oasis of calm doesn't take up much room, but it acts as a small reminder that self-care is always just a glance away.

Lighting is another important factor in making your workspace feel more inviting. Desk lamps with softer, warm light can make your space feel cozier and a bit less like a cubicle. Harsh fluorescent lighting can add to the stress (and, honestly, it doesn't make anyone look their best), but a desk lamp with a gentle glow can instantly change the mood. If your office doesn't allow personal lamps, try bringing in a small, battery-powered light. It's like a tiny hug for your eyes.

Adding Calming Scents can also make a big difference. A subtle lavender or eucalyptus spray can do wonders for your workspace. Just a spritz or two can refresh your mind and give your area a spa-like vibe. If you're in a shared workspace, be mindful not to overdo it— you don't want your desk neighbors wondering why your area suddenly smells like a forest. For a gentler approach, try a roll-on essential oil that you can apply to your wrists or dab on a tissue nearby.

One of the best ways to make your space feel calming is through Color and Texture. Add a few items in soothing colors—blues, greens, or neutral tones—to your desk. It could be as simple as a blue notebook, a green pen holder, or a soft gray mouse pad. These little touches of color and texture add a grounding element to your space, making it feel a bit more like home.

For a quick mental break, try placing a Comfort Object within reach. It could be a cozy blanket draped over your chair, a soft scarf, or even a plush pillow. Whenever you need a brief escape, reach for it and enjoy the comfort for a few seconds. It's like having a little piece of relaxation within arm's reach.

And finally, let's not overlook the power of Decluttering. It's tempting to let things pile up during busy times, but a messy workspace can lead to a messy mind. Take a few minutes each day to clear away papers, organize your pens, and wipe down your desk. A tidy space makes everything feel lighter, and you'll be surprised at how a clean desk can help clear your mind.

With these simple adjustments, you're transforming your workspace into a calm, inviting zone that supports focus and reduces stress. You don't need a total redesign; a few intentional touches are enough to make a difference. So go ahead and create a workspace that doesn't just work for you but works with you to help keep stress in check.

Transforming your workspace into a calm zone doesn't require a full remodel or a giant "self-care" banner hanging over your desk. With a few small tweaks—like adding a plant, soft lighting, or a quick declutter—you're setting yourself up for a day that feels less frantic and a bit more manageable. Now that you've got a calmer workspace let's see how you can bring that same peace to other parts of your daily routine. In the next chapter, we'll explore how to turn everyday chores into moments of calm, adding a touch of mindfulness to tasks you usually rush through. Ready to find zen in dishwashing and laundry? Let's dive in!

FOUR

Turning Daily Chores into Moments of Calm

Let's face it: chores are the unsung villains of adulthood. There's nothing thrilling about laundry; no one's lining up to scrub the sink. But what if you could turn these daily drudgeries into tiny opportunities for self-care? Yes, I'm serious—imagine folding towels as a path to inner peace or vacuuming as a shortcut to mental clarity. In this chapter, we will dive into ways to make even the dullest tasks feel a little more like "me time" and a little less like "why me?" chores. With a touch of mindfulness (and maybe a good playlist), you might find that zen hiding somewhere between the laundry pile and the junk drawer.

Finding Mindfulness in Household Tasks Like Dishwashing or Folding Laundry

Household chores: the little tasks we ignore until the laundry pile takes over the bedroom or the dishes start looking like modern art. But with a bit of creativity, these mundane tasks can actually become moments of calm—or at least less tedious. Think of them as sneaky opportunities to add a touch of zen to your day. After all, if you're going to spend time scrubbing or folding, you might as well get something out of it, right?

Let's start with dishwashing, which we can all agree ranks pretty low on the fun scale. Next time you're faced with a sink full of dishes, try to approach it as a mini meditation (yes, really). Instead of rushing through, focus on the warmth of the water, the softness of the bubbles, and the rhythm of scrubbing each dish. Picture each plate and mug like it's an ancient artifact you're restoring to its former glory. This isn't just washing dishes—it's a mindful experience. Feel free to throw in a deep sigh of wisdom as you rinse off that stubborn coffee stain. Who knew the kitchen sink could be such a sanctuary?

Laundry, too, has hidden potential for mindfulness. Folding clothes may seem repetitive, but it's oddly satisfying when you slow down and embrace it. Start with your space: find a cozy spot, put on a playlist or podcast, and get ready to tackle Mount Laundry. Each item you fold is like a tiny act of order, a chance to bring some calm to your day, one shirt at a time. You're not just folding; you're creating harmony, conquering chaos, and maybe even achieving inner peace through cotton blends. And at the end, you get the visual reward of neatly stacked clothes—proof that small victories exist.

Then there's vacuuming or sweeping. It might seem noisy, but there's something oddly satisfying about watching dust and crumbs disappear in real time. Try this trick: as you sweep or vacuum, imagine you're sweeping away stress and worries with each motion. Focus on the rhythmic back-and-forth, the hum of the vacuum, the lines forming on the carpet like a Zen garden (okay, maybe not quite, but close enough). You're not just cleaning; you're clearing space in your mind. Plus, when you finish, you're left with that rare feeling of satisfaction that only a crumb-free floor can bring.

For a bit of "advanced mindfulness," try organizing a drawer. We all have that one drawer—the "junk drawer" where everything goes when we don't know where else to put it. Instead of dreading it, turn organizing it into a little project. Take out each item, sort through the random pens, mystery keys, and outdated coupons, and give everything a home. There's something soothing about putting things in order, even if it's just one drawer. When you're done, you'll feel a small but undeniable sense of accomplishment. You didn't just organize; you conquered the clutter monster.

Of course, none of this is to say that chores will magically become your favorite activities. But with a sprinkle of mindfulness, they can feel like less of a hassle and more of a mental refresh. Think of each task as a micro-break for your mind, a chance to press "pause" on life's chaos and focus on something simple and repetitive. Plus, when you're done, you get the satisfaction of a cleaner space—a small, tangible reward that makes it all worth it (at least until next week).

So, next time you're looking at a pile of dishes, a mountain of laundry, or the infamous junk drawer, give these techniques a try. Slow down, pay attention to the details, and imagine each chore as a tiny act of self-care. You might still be scrubbing or folding, but at least you'll feel a little calmer and maybe—just maybe—a little more zen. Well, as zen as one can feel with a sponge in hand.

Tips for Making Cleaning Time Feel Like a Mental Break

Cleaning may not be anyone's idea of a dream afternoon, but what if you could trick yourself into enjoying it—at least a little? With a few tweaks, cleaning time can feel less like a chore and more like a mental break. We're talking relaxation, a hint of fun, and maybe even a touch of zen (yes, even when you're scrubbing the stove).

First off, cue the music. Think of it like creating a soundtrack for your very own cleaning montage. Whether you're into pop, rock, or a guilty pleasure '80s playlist, music can transform a dusting session into a full-blown jam. Imagine yourself in a movie scene as you swipe that mop across the floor with dramatic flair. If anyone catches you swaying with the broom, just say you're "embracing the rhythm of life." Bonus points if you lip-sync into a sponge—extra credit if you pull off an air guitar with a duster. Suddenly, cleaning feels like choreography, and who doesn't need a little more dance in their life?

If music doesn't quite do it, try listening to a podcast or audiobook. This is the perfect time to catch up on all those "must-listens" you've been saving. Suddenly, wiping down countertops becomes the perfect excuse to dive into a murder mystery or get free therapy advice from a self-help show. Mentally, you're not cleaning; you're out there solving crimes or learning how to "be your best self." It's multitasking at its finest: productive but in a way that feels almost... suspenseful. With each clean surface, you're a step closer to discovering the killer or finding inner peace.

For the aromatherapy fans out there, bring in some essential oils. A few drops of lavender, eucalyptus, or even lemon in your cleaning solution can transform your space into something that at least *smells* like a spa. Suddenly, scrubbing the bathroom feels a bit more luxurious (okay, maybe a stretch, but work with me here). Plus, essential oils have a knack for lifting your mood. Just be careful with the quantity—you want a gentle, refreshing scent, not a "Did someone spill a bottle of Pine-Sol?" situation. Your bathroom may end up smelling like a forest, but hey, that's better than smelling like last week's takeout, right?

If you're feeling up to the challenge, try mindful cleaning. Yes, I know: "mindful" and "cleaning" in the same sentence sounds a little ambitious, but stick with me. Focus on the details—feel the texture of the sponge, notice the shiny surface as you wipe, and listen to the satisfying spritz of the spray bottle. It's like a spa day for your senses, minus the fancy robe and cucumber water. By paying attention to each motion, you're not just cleaning; you're practicing a whole new level of self-care (or at least convincing yourself you are). It's almost meditative, and, who knows, you might find that wiping the counter is surprisingly...calming.

For those days when cleaning feels particularly daunting, create a reward system. Think of it as "bribing yourself." Promise yourself a treat after each task—a snack, a coffee, or even five minutes of guilt-free scrolling. The idea of a reward makes the whole ordeal feel like a game. You're not just scrubbing the sink; you're "working toward a goal" (aka that piece of chocolate waiting for you after the bathroom's sparkling clean). Who knew a snack could make cleaning feel so...motivating?

Finally, let's talk about the satisfaction factor. When you're done, take a moment to admire your work. Appreciate the shine, the fresh smell, and the fact that your space now looks like it's ready for a "before and after" post. Soak it in! Sure, it'll get messy again soon, but right now, you've created a little oasis of order in a chaotic world. It's a small victory, but it's all yours—enjoy it while it lasts. (And, if you really want, snap that "after" photo for yourself.)

By adding a bit of music, a favorite scent, or a well-earned reward, cleaning becomes less of a "must-do" and more of a mini-break. Who knows? With these little adjustments, you might even start looking forward to it... someday.

Creating Playlists or Podcasts to Make Chores Enjoyable

If there's one thing that can make chores tolerable—maybe even borderline fun—it's good entertainment. A playlist or podcast is like a secret ingredient that turns "ugh, laundry" into "I might as well finish this load so I can keep listening." With the right soundtrack, your chores can transform from dull to delightful. Or at least from "I'd rather not" to "Well, okay, fine."

Let's start with playlists. Music is the ultimate mood booster, and nothing says "I'm ready to conquer these dishes," like a playlist that makes you feel like a pop star in your kitchen. Think upbeat, danceable tracks that turn scrubbing and sweeping into a full-blown performance. Picture this: you, spinning around with a sponge, belting out lyrics into a spatula. Bonus points if your playlist includes a dramatic power ballad so you can really get into character while cleaning the oven. By the time you're done, you'll have cleaned up your kitchen *and* given yourself a mini concert experience.

If you're into something more relaxing, try a playlist of calming tunes. There's nothing quite like folding towels while listening to soft jazz or lo-fi beats. It almost feels like you're preparing for a day at the spa—except instead of facials, you're organizing the pantry. Still, the gentle background music can make even the most tedious tasks feel a little more serene. Just don't blame me if you get a sudden urge to light a candle and serve yourself a cucumber-infused glass of water.

For those who like a bit of adventure, consider making a "themed playlist." Think of it as creating a musical mood board for each chore. Doing laundry? Create a "Fresh and Clean" playlist with songs about being renewed, reborn, and free of stains. Scrubbing floors? Maybe you go for a "Hard Work" theme with classic rock or anthems that make you feel like you're tackling a Rocky-style training montage. These little themes add an element of fun and can make even the most mundane chore feel like it's part of a story arc.

Now, if music isn't quite enough, let's talk podcasts. Chores are the perfect time to catch up on episodes or dive into a new series. You're already folding or sweeping, so you might as well listen to a true crime mystery or an epic history podcast while you're at it. Suddenly, wiping down the fridge isn't just wiping down the fridge; it's something you're doing while solving a 20-year-old cold case. You're practically a detective now, and the fridge has never looked better.

If true crime feels a bit intense, try a comedy podcast. Laughter has a way of making time fly, and a good comedy show can turn vacuuming into a lighthearted break. It's hard to resent dusting when you're busy laughing at someone's hilarious take on the horrors of adulting. You'll be wiping windows, laughing at jokes, and wondering why you haven't tried this sooner. By the time you finish, you'll feel like you just hung out with friends without leaving your house.

For a bit of self-improvement, choose a motivational or self-help podcast. Picture yourself cleaning and *bettering* yourself at the same time. You'll be sweeping floors while mentally preparing to conquer your goals, decluttering your life and your mind. It's multitasking at its finest: clean counters and newfound wisdom.

If you're indecisive, mix it up: create a playlist of songs and snippets of podcasts, giving you the best of both worlds. One minute, you're grooving to your favorite song, and the next, you're learning a random fun fact that makes you think, "I really should bring that up in conversation." Who knew cleaning could make you the most interesting person at the next dinner party?

At the end of the day, playlists and podcasts are like magic potions for chores. They add a dash of enjoyment, a sprinkle of distraction, and turn ordinary tasks into something worth looking forward to—okay, maybe "looking forward to" is a stretch, but you get the idea. Give it a try, and you might find that with the right audio, even chores can be...dare I say, enjoyable.

Turning Organizing Tasks into "Brain Breaks"

Organizing can sometimes feel like the ultimate "I'll get to it later" task. But what if you could trick your brain into seeing it as a break? With the right mindset, a little organizing can feel less like work and more like a mini-refresh—a "brain break" that brings order to your space *and* your mind. Think of it as a way to declutter your life, one sock drawer at a time.

Start small, like with that infamous junk drawer. You know the one: a collection of random pens, spare keys, expired coupons, and a mysterious charger that probably belongs to a device from 2010. Tackling a single drawer can be surprisingly satisfying. Dump it out, give yourself five minutes, and start sorting. Suddenly, you're not just organizing; you're discovering lost treasures (and wondering why you kept them). By the time you're done, you'll have transformed chaos into order. Plus, you'll get a little mental boost from knowing that, for once, you know exactly where the scissors are.

If you're feeling more ambitious, try tackling your desk. Desks have a sneaky way of collecting clutter—papers, pens, receipts, and at least one or two snacks for emergencies. Take a few minutes to put everything in its rightful place, maybe even wipe down the surface for an extra "fresh start" vibe. This isn't just about aesthetics; clearing off your desk can actually make it easier to focus. Less visual clutter = less mental clutter. It's like giving your brain a breather. Now, when you sit down to work, you'll feel a little more organized and a lot less overwhelmed.

Closets are another organizing goldmine. They're like the hidden caverns of our homes, filled with forgotten items and questionable fashion choices. Pick one small section—shoes, jackets, or that shelf full of "I swear I'll wear this someday" items—and give it a quick overhaul. Donate, sort, and reorganize. Not only will you feel a sense of accomplishment, but you'll also rediscover clothes you forgot you owned. It's like shopping without spending a dime. By the time you're done, you'll feel like you've accomplished something big—and the next time you open the closet, it won't look like a hurricane just passed through.

If you're really in the mood to refresh, try organizing your digital space. Yep, your computer desktop could probably use a little love. Start with the basics: delete old files, organize folders, and clear out any random screenshots. Think of it as "spring cleaning" for your laptop. When your screen is clean and clutter-free, logging on suddenly feels a little less stressful. You might even find yourself feeling oddly professional, like the kind of person who has their life together—even if it's just digital.

For a quick win, tackle your wallet or purse. Take out the old receipts, expired coupons, and random scraps of paper. Organize your cards and maybe even toss in a fresh stick of gum or a little hand sanitizer. It's a tiny task, but the next time you reach for your wallet, you'll feel like you have your life together—even if your only plan is a trip to the grocery store. It's these little touches that make organization feel like a quick mental pick-me-up.

These organizing tasks don't need to be big, exhausting projects. In fact, the smaller, quicker tasks can be the most satisfying. Each little piece of organization adds a dose of calm to your life, and you get that satisfying feeling of "Hey, I did something productive." Plus, by treating these tasks as "brain breaks," you're tricking yourself into thinking they're a refreshing break from your regular routine. You're not just organizing; you're giving yourself a little mental reset, one drawer or desktop folder at a time.

So, next time you need a mental break, skip the social media scroll and try a quick organizing task instead. In just a few minutes, you'll have decluttered your space and, in the process, refreshed your mind. Who knew tidying up could feel this rewarding?

From creating playlists that make you want to dance with the broom to turning the junk drawer into a mini treasure hunt, these everyday tasks aren't just chores—they're hidden opportunities for relaxation and a mental refresh. Now that we've tackled how to find peace within the chaos of daily tasks, it's time to slow down even more. In the next chapter, we'll explore how mealtime can become another moment for self-care, helping you savor each bite and make even quick meals feel a little more meaningful. Ready to turn eating into an art of mindfulness? Let's dig in!

FIVE

Meal Times as Mindful Moments

For many of us, mealtime has become a speed-eating contest we didn't sign up for. Whether it's lunch at your desk, dinner on the couch, or breakfast while sprinting out the door, food has become more about "fuel" than "flavor." But here's a twist: what if eating didn't have to feel like a pit stop? With a bit of mindfulness, you can turn even the busiest meal into a mini-vacation—a small, satisfying break where you actually taste your food. This chapter is all about slowing down, savoring each bite, and making mealtime feel less like a chore and more like a moment of self-care. Ready to rediscover the joy of eating? Forks up!

Quick, Easy Recipes That Are Nutritious and Low-Stress

We all want to eat healthy, delicious meals, but who has time for elaborate recipes? If the average recipe has you chopping, sautéing, and juggling ten different ingredients, it can feel easier to just order takeout and call it a day. But with a few simple recipes up your sleeve, you can whip up nutritious meals without the fuss, drama, or kitchen disaster potential.

Let's start with *The 5-Minute Salad That Doesn't Suck.* Salads have a bad reputation for being boring, but this one is a little different. Start with a handful of mixed greens, toss in some cherry tomatoes (pre-washed because we're aiming for easy here), add a few slices of cucumber, and throw on a sprinkle of shredded carrots. Now, for the pièce de résistance, add some pre-cooked rotisserie chicken or a scoop of chickpeas. Drizzle a little olive oil and balsamic vinegar on top, and boom! You have a salad that's fresh, filling, and requires zero culinary skills. No sad, wilted lettuce here—just a bowl of health that took less time to make than it did to read this paragraph.

Next up is *The Lazy Omelette,* a perfect choice when you want a warm meal but don't want to babysit a pan. Crack a couple of eggs into a bowl, whisk them with a fork, and pour them into a preheated pan. Add a handful of spinach or whatever random vegetables are in your fridge, sprinkle with cheese, and let it cook until it's just set. Slide it onto a plate, fold it in half (for that fancy omelet look), and voila—a nutritious breakfast, lunch, or dinner with practically no effort. You'll look like a chef even though you're just tossing together eggs and whatever's left in the crisper.

For dinner, consider *The Sheet Pan Miracle.* It's exactly what it sounds like: throw everything on a baking sheet, stick it in the oven, and let it handle itself. Start with some chopped veggies—think bell peppers, carrots, or broccoli—add a protein like chicken breasts or chickpeas, and drizzle with olive oil, salt, and pepper. Roast at 400°F for about 20-30 minutes. The beauty of this meal is that it's nearly impossible to mess up. And as a bonus, you only have one pan to clean. Serve it over rice, quinoa, or salad greens if you want to make it even more filling. It's low-stress, low-mess, and tastes way better than you'd expect from something so simple.

For the ultimate lazy day meal, there's *The No-Cook Wrap.* Grab a whole-wheat tortilla, spread some hummus or Greek yogurt on it, add pre-washed greens, shredded carrots, a handful of shredded rotisserie chicken or tofu, and roll it up. It's a wrap; it's done, and there's no cooking involved. Think of it as the ultimate desk-friendly lunch or dinner, ready in seconds and customizable with whatever you've got lying around. Plus, you can make two, wrap one for later, and congratulate yourself on tomorrow's meal being done early.

And if you're craving something sweet but healthy, *The 3-Ingredient Smoothie* is your go-to. Blend a frozen banana, a cup of almond milk (or whatever milk you like), and a handful of spinach for a surprisingly tasty, nutrient-packed drink. Want to jazz it up? Add a scoop of protein powder or a spoonful of peanut butter. You'll be sipping a smoothie that tastes way better than "health food" should.

With these recipes, you're armed with quick, nutritious meals that don't require culinary expertise or hours in the kitchen. Think of them as your go-to options for when you want to eat well without sacrificing precious free time—or sanity. Give them a try, and you might just discover that "cooking" doesn't have to be a chore.

How to Slow Down at Mealtime, Even with a Packed Schedule

If you're used to inhaling meals like they're part of a competitive eating contest, the idea of slowing down might sound impossible. Between work, family, and that endless to-do list, taking a "relaxed" approach to eating can feel like a luxury. But slowing down at mealtime doesn't require hours—it's about making a few small adjustments that let you enjoy your food, even on the busiest days.

Let's start with the simplest trick: *Put Down the Fork.* I know it sounds obvious, but hear me out. After every bite, make a point of actually setting your fork down for a second. This micro-pause gives you a chance to chew, breathe, and actually taste what you're eating. You don't have to put down the fork for long—just a second or two. Think of it as a little breather between bites, like a mini-vacation for your mouth. Plus, it's way harder to overeat when you're not just shoveling food in.

Next, try *The Two-Bite Technique*. Take two bites, then pause to check in with yourself. How's the food? Are you actually enjoying it? Are you already full? This little mental check-in lets you slow down and stay mindful of your hunger cues. It also gives you a second to appreciate what you're eating, which, let's be honest, we don't often do when we're in rush mode. And if your brain is yelling, "Keep eating, it's delicious!" that's totally fine—at least you're present with your food instead of treating it like fuel you're tossing back to get on with life.

For a more structured approach, consider setting a *Timer Challenge*. This one's especially helpful if you tend to devour meals in five minutes or less. Set a timer for ten minutes, and challenge yourself to make the meal last until it goes off. You don't have to sit there staring at the clock but use the timer as a gentle reminder to pace yourself. Think of it as turning mealtime into a little game. The goal? Finish your plate slowly, savoring each bite, and, for once, not finishing before the microwave chime has even faded.

If you're eating with others, make *Conversation the Main Dish*. The more you talk, the less you can rush through your food. Use the meal as a chance to catch up, share a laugh, or even just discuss that new show everyone's watching. It's a natural way to slow down because you'll be taking breaks between bites as you talk. If you're dining solo, consider a little self-conversation (okay, maybe keep it internal) about how your day's going or how you're feeling about the food. It sounds silly, but taking a moment to pause and reflect—even mentally— helps you engage with the meal rather than just racing through it.

Another easy tactic is *Eat with Your Non-Dominant Hand*. Switching hands makes eating a bit more challenging, forcing you to slow down. Yes, it feels weird at first, but it's a great trick to prevent mindless munching. You'll be surprised at how much longer it takes to finish a meal when you're awkwardly fumbling with a fork in your left hand (or right if you're left-handed). Plus, it makes mealtime a bit of an adventure, which is a nice twist if your routine has gotten a little stale.

Finally, try *Savoring Just One Bite*. Before you dive into the meal, focus on a single bite. Chew slowly, noticing the flavors, textures, and spices. You don't have to do this for the entire meal, but just one intentional bite can set the tone for a slower, more enjoyable experience. It's like priming your brain to appreciate the food rather than just consume it. You're giving yourself permission to relax, even if it's just for a moment.

With these tips, slowing down at mealtime is doable, even on a packed schedule. Give yourself permission to pause, savor, and enjoy. Your food—and your stress levels—will thank you.

Ideas for Mindful Eating and Savoring Each Bite

In a world where "lunch" often means scarfing down a sandwich while answering emails, the concept of mindful eating can feel a little... aspirational. But the good news is you don't need a full meditation retreat to savor your food. With a few small tweaks, you can make each bite a bit more meaningful—even if you're dining at your desk or squeezing in a snack between errands.

One of the easiest ways to start is with *The Single-Bite Appreciation*. Before you dive into your meal, pick one bite to savor. Take it slowly, noticing the textures, the flavors, and even the temperature. Is it crunchy? Creamy? Sweet? Salty? This single, focused bite primes your brain to pay attention to the rest of the meal. Think of it like a warm-up for your taste buds, a little pre-game ritual for your appetite.

If you're ready to take it up a notch, try *The Chew-20-Times Challenge.* For each bite, chew at least 20 times before swallowing. This sounds a little excessive, but it's a game-changer. Not only does it make you slow down, but it also lets you taste your food in ways you might miss when you're eating quickly. Plus, you'll feel fuller faster, which means less chance of overeating. And yes, you'll probably realize that chewing 20 times feels ridiculous at first, but give it a shot. By the third bite, you'll feel like a mindful-eating pro.

Another trick is *The Eyes-Closed Bite.* This one's a bit out there but stick with me. Closing your eyes while you take a bite cuts out the distractions and lets you focus on the flavors. It's like giving your taste buds the spotlight, just for a second. Now, if you're at a fancy restaurant or in a crowded break room, this might feel a little weird—maybe try it at home first. But trust me, it's worth it. By blocking out visual noise, you'll notice subtle flavors you might otherwise miss.

To add even more mindfulness, try *The Food Origin Story.* As you eat, take a second to think about where each ingredient came from. Imagine the journey of the tomato in your salad, the cheese in your sandwich, or the rice in your bowl. Visualize the farm, the field, or even the grocery aisle. No need for a full history lesson, but a quick mental "thank you" to the people and places that brought your meal to life adds a layer of appreciation. It's like giving your meal a backstory, which makes it a little more interesting and a lot more enjoyable.

Another fun approach is *The Flavors Detective.* With each bite, try to pinpoint specific flavors or spices. Is that a hint of garlic? A dash of pepper? Or maybe a subtle sweetness you didn't notice at first? Tuning into the individual flavors lets you fully experience the meal instead of just shoveling it down. It's a bit like solving a delicious mystery, one bite at a time. Plus, you'll feel like a mini food critic, which makes eating feel a lot more special than usual.

For a quick and easy way to slow down, use *The Tiny Utensil Trick*. Yes, I'm suggesting you use a smaller fork or spoon. When your utensil is smaller, you naturally take smaller bites, which forces you to slow down and pay more attention to each mouthful. You'll be savoring each bite, partly because it's hard not to when you're taking micro-nibbles. Plus, using a tiny fork is oddly satisfying—it's like turning mealtime into a miniature feast.

Finally, consider setting *An Eating Intention*. Before you start, take a second to mentally decide how you want the meal to feel. Maybe it's "I'm going to enjoy every bite" or "I'll eat slowly and stop when I'm satisfied." This little mental note keeps you connected to the experience, reminding you that this is your time to eat, not rush.

Mindful eating doesn't have to be complicated. With these simple tricks, you'll find yourself slowing down, savoring flavors, and enjoying food in a whole new way. So next time you sit down for a meal, take a few deep breaths, bring out the tiny fork, and give your taste buds the attention they deserve.

Ways to Make Eating Healthy Feel Effortless

Eating healthy sounds great in theory, but the reality can feel like a never-ending quest for kale and quinoa. The good news? Healthy eating doesn't have to be complicated, time-consuming, or taste like cardboard. With a few tricks, you can make healthy choices feel natural, easy, and, yes, even enjoyable—no fancy superfoods required.

First up is *The Power of Prepping (Without Becoming a Meal Prep Maniac)*. The idea of meal prep usually brings to mind rows of identical containers filled with chicken and broccoli. But meal prep doesn't need to be intense! Start small by prepping a few basics: wash and chop veggies for salads, cook a pot of quinoa or rice, or bake a batch of chicken breasts. These staples give you a foundation, so when hunger strikes, you're halfway to a healthy meal. Bonus: you can still feel like a meal-prepping pro without spending your entire Sunday in the kitchen.

For days when you're low on energy, try *The Art of the Shortcut*. Pre-washed greens, frozen veggies, and rotisserie chicken are lifesavers here. Stock up on a few of these "cheat" ingredients to make throwing together a healthy meal as easy as possible. Think of it as assembling rather than cooking—mix pre-washed greens with rotisserie chicken, add a scoop of hummus, and you're done. With these shortcuts, you can eat well without chopping, dicing, or even turning on the stove.

If you're aiming for balance without the headache, use *The Plate Method*. Just divide your plate into sections: half should be veggies, a quarter protein, and a quarter carbs. Voilà! Instant portion control without math or calorie counting. It's a visual cheat sheet for balanced eating—just fill in the sections, and you're good to go. Plus, this method lets you mix and match foods however you like, making meals feel less like a chore and more like a creative exercise.

To make healthy eating even easier, embrace *The One-Bowl Wonders*. Bowls are the best thing to happen to fast, healthy meals. Grab a bowl, add a base like rice or greens, top it with whatever veggies and protein you have, sprinkle on some nuts or seeds, and drizzle a quick dressing over it. Bowls are the "choose your own adventure" of meals. They're adaptable, filling, and incredibly easy to throw together. And there's something about eating from a bowl that feels comforting, even if it's packed with veggies.

When you're in the mood to snack, try *Smart Snacking (AKA Out of Sight, Out of Mouth)*. Keep healthy snacks like nuts, fruit, or yogurt within reach, and store the tempting stuff (chips, cookies, etc.) somewhere less obvious. If you have to go looking for the bag of chips, you're less likely to grab it impulsively. By making healthy snacks the easiest option, you're setting yourself up to make better choices without even thinking about it. It's like fooling yourself into healthy eating—no willpower required.

Another trick for effortless healthy eating is *Batch Dressing*. Salads get a bad rap because, let's be honest, a dry salad is nobody's idea of fun. Take five minutes to whip up a batch of dressing at the beginning of the week. Store it in a jar in the fridge, and you'll have tasty dressing ready to go for any salad emergency. A quick drizzle of homemade vinaigrette can make even the most basic greens feel fancy, turning salad from "ugh" to "yum" with minimal effort.

Finally, remember the golden rule of eating healthy: *Progress, Not Perfection*. It's about balance. Eating healthy doesn't mean you can't have treats—it just means focusing on nourishing choices most of the time. By keeping it simple, you'll find that healthy eating can fit seamlessly into your routine. No complicated recipes, no guilt—just easy, enjoyable meals that make you feel good.

With these tricks, you'll be surprised at how natural and stress-free healthy eating can be. So stock up on some pre-washed greens, set out a few bowls, and make healthy choices feel less like a chore and more like second nature.

Healthy eating doesn't need to be an ordeal, and mealtime can actually become a moment of calm in a busy day. With quick, balanced recipes, simple ways to savor each bite, and easy meal-prep tricks, eating well can feel natural—even enjoyable! Now that we've covered how to bring mindfulness and health to the table, it's time to look at those well-deserved breaks in front of the TV. In the next chapter, we'll dive into how to turn screen time into a meaningful way to unwind, making it feel less like a habit and more like a relaxing ritual. Ready to put your feet up and make your binge-watching sessions count? Grab the remote, and let's explore.

SIX

Self-Care in Front of the TV: Making Screen Time Meaningful

Let's be honest: for many of us, unwinding in front of the TV is a sacred ritual. Whether it's a favorite show, a comforting movie, or a guilty pleasure reality series, screen time can be an easy way to decompress. But what if it could be even more relaxing, even more refreshing? In this chapter, we'll look at ways to make TV time feel like a self-care experience, turning your usual binge-watching session into something that helps you truly unwind. From mindful viewing habits to setting the scene, we're going to turn screen time into quality "me time"—no remote hogging required.

Turning Screen Time into Relaxation Time with Mindful Viewing

Let's be real—TV time is sacred. It's the chance to zone out, tune in, and sometimes forget that laundry is waiting. But there's a big difference between letting Netflix run on autopilot and actually turning TV time into a self-care ritual. With a few tweaks, you can make your screen time feel like an actual recharge instead of just a habit.

First, *Choose Wisely.* Just because something's trending doesn't mean it's the right show for your mood. Want to laugh? Skip the dark dramas and go straight for that ridiculous comedy you've seen ten times. Feeling the need for a mental vacation? Watch a show set in a sunny location where no one's ever heard of a to-do list. Picking your show like you'd pick a vacation destination makes the experience feel intentional and a lot less like you're just watching whatever the algorithm throws your way.

Now that you've made your choice, try this: *The No-Multitasking Rule.* I know it's tempting to scroll, snack, and answer emails while "watching," but multitasking is just robbing you of the chance to actually relax. For this session, consider the TV as the only task. Imagine you're in a movie theater where taking out your phone would result in immediate judgment. The goal is to get absorbed in the story, not to also be 40% focused on emails. You'll find that single-tasking actually lets you enjoy the show as if it were your first time discovering TV.

To set the right mood, *Create a Cozy Scene.* You don't have to go full interior decorator here, but little touches make a big difference. Dim the lights, grab a fluffy blanket, and maybe even light a candle for some added ambiance. You're not just "watching TV"; you're entering a mini spa experience with a side of entertainment. Think of it as turning your living room into a movie theater, minus the popcorn line and the person loudly unwrapping candy beside you.

When watching a series, consider *The One-Episode Pause.* The binge-watch urge is strong, but taking a break between episodes helps keep the enjoyment alive. Pause, stretch, maybe grab a snack or do a victory lap around the room. Then, settle back in for the next episode with renewed enthusiasm. You're not speed-running the entire season in one sitting; you're savoring each episode like a fine wine—well, a fine wine that sometimes involves superheroes or crime-solving pets.

For added relaxation, use *Reflective Moments*. This doesn't mean writing a thesis on the show's themes, but take a second to appreciate what you're watching. Did something make you laugh? Remind you of something silly? These tiny check-ins make you more connected with the experience. It's like adding mindfulness to your binge-watching—you'll remember the best moments instead of the vague blur that sometimes follows a marathon session.

Lastly, don't underestimate the power of *Rewatching Old Favorites*. Sometimes, nothing is more relaxing than a show where you already know every plot twist. Rewatching a favorite show is like having an old friend over—you're already comfortable, you know what's coming, and there's zero stress. Let the nostalgia wash over you as you get lost in the familiar storyline. You're not watching to be surprised; you're watching to feel all the warm fuzzies of familiarity.

With a bit of mindful viewing, screen time can be more than zoning out. Instead of letting episodes blend together, pick something that suits your mood, set the scene, and savor the experience. By the end, you'll feel less like you've been hypnotized by your TV and more like you've actually had a chance to unwind. So next time you reach for the remote, give these tricks a try—you might just find that screen time can be the ultimate mini-vacation.

Ideas for a "Wind-Down" Routine Before and After Watching TV

We often treat TV like an instant "on" switch for relaxation, flipping it on the second we collapse onto the couch. But with a little wind-down routine before and after, you can make your screen time even more relaxing—like a TV-watching ritual that's about more than just hitting play. These small pre- and post-TV habits can make the experience feel like a well-earned treat instead of just default downtime.

First, there's *The Pre-Show Setup.* This is your chance to prepare for a relaxing viewing experience, setting the scene just right. Grab your favorite blanket, adjust the lighting, and if you're feeling extra fancy, make a little snack. Imagine you're at an exclusive movie premiere, except the star is your favorite show, and the red carpet is your couch. A quick setup like this sends a signal to your brain that it's time to relax—and when you finally hit play, you're not just watching TV; you're indulging in a mini-event.

Then there's *The Pre-Show Stretch.* This one's simple: before you settle in, take a minute to stretch. A few shoulder rolls, maybe a quick neck stretch, or a touch-your-toes attempt if you're feeling ambitious. It's a small, subtle way to release some tension before you dive into couch mode. Plus, a little movement means you won't feel quite so couch-potato-ish after a long watching session.

Once you're ready to start, consider *The Intentional First Episode.* Don't just hit play—take a deep breath, settle in, and let yourself get fully absorbed in the show. By making the first episode feel like the main event, you're setting the tone for the rest of your TV time. It's like saying to yourself, "Okay, this is *my* time, and I'm going to enjoy every second of it." You'll feel more relaxed and focused like you're watching with purpose instead of letting the episodes play on autopilot.

After the show ends, it's time for *The Post-Show Breather.* Resist the urge to jump up and get back to tasks right away. Instead, sit back for a minute, let the credits roll, and take a few deep breaths. Reflect on what you just watched—was it funny, surprising, or just plain silly? Give yourself a moment to savor the experience before rushing off to the next thing. Think of it as a cool-down period, like a stretch for your mind after your show-marathon workout.

If you're finishing a whole series or movie, consider *The Quick Stroll.* Going for a short walk (even if it's just to the kitchen and back) after screen time helps shake off the "TV trance" and gives your eyes a break. Plus, a little movement is a nice way to let your brain process what you watched. Whether you're mulling over a plot twist or laughing at that ridiculous scene, the mini stroll makes your screen time feel more like an event that you're actually wrapping up rather than something that just... ends.

For a bit of bedtime TV, add *The Digital Dimmer* to your routine. Most devices now have a night mode that reduces blue light, which can help ease your eyes into relaxation mode before sleep. Switch on night mode to make watching TV a little more sleep-friendly. It's like turning your screen into a candle-lit version of itself, softening the glow and making your eyes feel less like they're staring at a spotlight.

Lastly, finish with *The Post-Show Refill.* Hydrate before and after a screen session; it's easy to get dehydrated when you're cozy on the couch. Keep a glass of water nearby, and take a sip between episodes or after you finish. It's a simple way to keep yourself refreshed, and it'll make that post-TV transition feel a little more like a "wrap-up" than a sudden halt.

With these wind-down tips, screen time becomes more than just a habit. You're creating a relaxed, purposeful viewing experience that feels both enjoyable and refreshing. So next time you turn on the TV, try adding a pre- and post-show ritual to make the most of every relaxing moment. You're not just watching TV—you're mastering the art of couch relaxation.

How to Use Ad Breaks as Quick Self-Care Moments

Ad breaks are usually the time we endure with a sigh, waiting impatiently to get back to the show. But what if these pesky interruptions could actually work in your favor? Instead of scrolling aimlessly or impatiently waiting for the countdown to hit zero, ad breaks can become your mini self-care pit stops. With a little creativity, these few minutes can be used for quick recharges, leaving you feeling more refreshed by the time the show resumes.

First, try *The Quick Stretch*. It's simple: when the ads start, get up and stretch. Roll your shoulders, stretch your neck, or reach for the sky like you're warming up for an Olympic event (even if it's just an event in lounging). A quick stretch can release some of the tension that builds up while sitting, especially if you're settling in for a longer binge-watch session. Plus, it's like a little gift to your body in exchange for all that sitting.

For a boost of energy, go for *The Ad Break Hydration*. Grab a glass of water or make yourself a quick cup of tea. Staying hydrated while watching TV is a sneaky form of self-care that's super easy to overlook. Plus, the walk to the kitchen doubles as a quick mini-break. By the time you get back to the couch with your drink, you'll feel a little more awake and refreshed—no mid-episode yawning here!

Another idea is *The 30-Second Tidy*. Use the ad time to tidy up the space around you. Fold that blanket, fluff up the pillows, or stack up any scattered magazines or dishes. You'd be surprised at how much a quick spruce-up can make your environment feel more pleasant. It's like a mini makeover for your viewing area, and it feels oddly satisfying to have a freshened-up space by the time the show's back on.

For a bit of mental relaxation, try *The Breathing Break*. Sit back, close your eyes, and take a few deep breaths. Inhale for four counts, hold for four, exhale for four, and repeat. It's the ultimate "I'm on a quick vacation" vibe, even if you're just sitting in your living room. With just a few deep breaths, you're grounding yourself and clearing your mind. By the time the show's back, you'll feel more relaxed, like you've just had a mini spa experience without leaving the couch.

Another creative option is *The Gratitude Glance*. During the ad break, look around and think of one or two things you're grateful for in that moment. It could be the comfy couch you're lounging on, the cozy blanket wrapped around you, or even just the fact that you have this time to unwind. This quick mental check-in doesn't take much time, but it can add a touch of positivity to your TV-watching session. Suddenly, it's not just screen time—it's gratitude time.

If you're watching with family or friends, try *The Quick Chat*. Ad breaks are perfect for a quick catch-up—no need for deep conversations, just a few fun comments or a laugh over the last scene. It's a small way to connect with the people you're watching with and enjoy the experience together. Plus, it keeps the mood light and lively, so you're not all just staring blankly until the show resumes.

Lastly, for a touch of productivity, try *The Micro-Task*. Tackle one small to-do from your list during each ad break—maybe it's responding to a quick text, setting an alarm, or making a grocery list. Keep it simple and short so it doesn't feel like "work." It's like sneaking in a bit of productivity, so when the show's over, you're not left with a mountain of to-dos. Plus, you'll feel like a multitasking wizard by the end of the episode.

With these ideas, ad breaks become more than just interruptions. They're opportunities for a quick reset, leaving you feeling energized and refreshed by the time the show's back on. So, next time the ads roll around, try a little self-care pit stop. You'll thank yourself when the episode ends, and you feel just as relaxed as you hoped.

TV Shows That Inspire Calm, Positivity, or Mindfulness

Sometimes, we turn to TV not just for entertainment but for a much-needed dose of calm or positivity. Luckily, there's a whole lineup of shows out there that go beyond drama and thrill—they're designed to lift your spirits, bring a sense of peace, or just make you feel all-around good. Think of these as the comfort food of television, except without the calories or the guilt.

First on the list: *Nature Documentaries*. Few things are as calming as watching breathtaking shots of oceans, forests, and cute baby animals —especially when narrated by a soothing voice. Whether it's David Attenborough or the smooth tones of Sigourney Weaver, nature docs are like a spa day for your brain. Watching dolphins play or plants bloom in time-lapse reminds you that the world is still full of beauty and wonder, even if your email inbox says otherwise. You can't help but feel a little more zen as you immerse yourself in the wonders of the natural world.

For a hit of positivity, look no further than *Feel-Good Cooking Shows*. Shows like *The Great British Bake Off* have perfected the art of gentle competition. Instead of intense, high-stakes battles, you get polite contestants, delicious pastries, and a complete lack of sabotage. It's all about cakes, camaraderie, and constructive criticism, and somehow, it's the most relaxing viewing experience ever. Watching people gently knead dough and decorate cookies with utmost care is oddly therapeutic, even if you have no intention of baking yourself.

If cooking isn't your jam, consider *Makeover and Home Improvement Shows*. Shows like *Queer Eye* or *Tidying Up with Marie Kondo* go beyond the superficial; they're all about bringing a sense of joy and peace to people's lives. Watching someone rediscover happiness in their revamped space or confidently embrace a new style can leave you feeling warm and fuzzy. And who doesn't love a good transformation? It's like watching a caterpillar become a butterfly—except with better lighting and before-and-after shots.

For those who want a little mindfulness, *Slow TV* is surprisingly calming. Imagine watching a scenic train ride through Norway or a boat journey down a river—all in real time. Yes, it's hours of watching scenery go by, and it sounds boring, but that's exactly what makes it so relaxing. There's no plot, no drama, and no intense music cueing a big reveal. It's just you, the train, and the slow, steady movement through landscapes. It's a mindful experience that's practically meditation for your TV screen.

If you're looking for something uplifting and full of good vibes, *Heartwarming Reality Shows* are a great choice. Shows like *Kindness Diaries* follow people who travel around the world, relying on the kindness of strangers or those that highlight acts of generosity and compassion. These shows are a reminder that there's plenty of good in the world, and they tend to leave you feeling hopeful about humanity. It's feel-good TV that doesn't shy away from emotion, so don't be surprised if you get a little misty-eyed.

For pure, laugh-out-loud positivity, there's nothing like a classic *Sitcom*. Shows like *Parks and Recreation* or *The Office* offer light-hearted humor and quirky characters that become like old friends. With episodes that wrap up in 20 minutes, you get a quick hit of laughs, a bit of warmth, and no serious emotional investment. It's easygoing TV at its finest, perfect for unwinding after a long day.

Whether you're in need of calm, positivity, or a bit of both, these shows bring more than just entertainment to the screen—they bring a little extra joy, peace, or mindfulness to your day. So, the next time you need a break, turn to one of these options and enjoy some quality time in front of the TV, knowing you're getting a dose of good vibes along with your favorite snacks.

TV can be more than just background noise or a quick way to unwind—it can actually become a source of calm, positivity, and even mindfulness with the right choices. From transforming ad breaks into mini self-care sessions to watching shows that uplift and inspire, screen time doesn't have to be mindless. Now that we've covered how to make your TV time a true relaxation ritual let's shift to the end of the day. In the next chapter, we'll dive into evening wind-down routines that help you let go of the day's stress and prepare for a restful night. Get ready to relax and recharge as we explore the art of winding down.

SEVEN

Evening Wind-Down Routines for a Restful Night

After a long day, winding down can feel like a mythical concept. Often, we rely on the classic "collapse into bed" technique and hope sleep will follow. But with a few simple routines, bedtime can become a relaxing ritual rather than a last-minute scramble. This chapter will cover easy evening habits that gently transition you from the day's buzz into pure calm. Whether it's a quick gratitude practice or a breathing technique, these routines will help make hitting the pillow feel like the reward it's meant to be.

Short Evening Rituals to Transition from Work Mode to Relaxation

Switching off after a full day isn't always easy. Sometimes it feels like the brain insists on clinging to that last email or replaying a meeting in your head on repeat. But a few small, purposeful habits can help you unwind and convince your mind that, yes, work is truly over for the day.

One tried-and-true trick is *The Mini Room Reset*. Pick one area of your home—ideally where you relax, like the living room or bedroom—and give it a quick tidy-up. This doesn't mean deep cleaning or reorganizing furniture; think more like fluffing pillows, folding the throw blanket, or putting away random clutter. The goal here is simple: when the room looks calm, your mind feels a little calmer, too. Plus, the ritual of tidying up just one spot acts as a symbolic "closing time" for your day.

Next is *The Work Clothes Swap*. There's something strangely powerful about changing out of your "work" clothes, even if you're working from home in something halfway between pajamas and a conference-ready outfit. Put on whatever feels softest, comfiest, and least like something you'd wear to a meeting. It's like signaling to your body, "Okay, we're officially off-duty." Even the act of slipping into fuzzy socks or an oversized hoodie can do wonders for the mind. Suddenly, productivity mode takes a back seat, and relaxation is ready to take the wheel.

For a quick mental breather, try *The "Day's Done" Reflection*. Take a minute to look back on the day—just a quick recap, nothing too serious. Mentally acknowledge what went well, maybe note anything funny that happened, or give yourself a pat on the back for surviving the day's challenges. If something went wrong, allow yourself to let it go, reminding yourself that it's now tomorrow's problem (if it's still a problem at all). This tiny recap helps you mentally file away the day so you're not dragging it to bed with you.

A personal favorite of many is *The Screen Swap*. About 30 minutes before bed, trade out the phone or laptop for a book, a magazine, or even an old-school puzzle. Studies show that blue light from screens can mess with sleep, so putting the screens down actually helps signal to your brain that it's time to wind down. And besides, there's something pleasantly low-tech about flipping through a book or doing a crossword puzzle. Plus, if you fall asleep halfway through a sentence, it feels more poetic than just conking out mid-scroll.

For a touch of calm, try *The Gratitude Glance*. Before you head to bed, take a moment to reflect on a few things you're grateful for. These don't need to be grand achievements—think about small moments from your day, like enjoying your morning coffee, getting a funny text, or simply finding a good parking spot. This quick gratitude check-in shifts your mindset away from stress and into a more peaceful state. And if nothing else, it'll add a little positivity to your evening, helping you drift off with better vibes.

Finally, wrap it all up with *The Relaxation Cue*. Choose one last little ritual that tells your brain it's officially bedtime. This could be dimming the lights, playing soft music, or spritzing a little lavender spray on your pillow. The goal is to set a relaxing tone, creating a sense of calm that helps signal to your body that the day is done. This final cue reinforces the idea that you're off-duty, easing you gently into the night.

With these simple evening rituals, unwinding at the end of the day feels a little less elusive. They're quick and low-effort, but they help bridge the gap between work mode and bedtime, easing you out of the day's stress and into relaxation.

Ways to Practice Gratitude Before Bed Without Adding Stress

Gratitude before bed can be a game-changer for relaxation. But let's be honest—at the end of a long day, no one's in the mood to write a three-page list of "Things I'm Grateful For." Luckily, gratitude doesn't have to be complicated, time-consuming, or involve journaling marathons. With a few easy approaches, you can add a touch of gratitude to your bedtime routine without it feeling like a chore.

First up, try *The One-Thing Method.* This is gratitude in its simplest form: before you settle in, think of just one thing from your day that you're thankful for. It can be as small as finding a great parking spot, catching a beautiful sunset, or having an especially satisfying snack. No need to dig deep or search for profound moments—just pick something that genuinely made you smile, even if it was only for a few seconds. This little reflection takes almost no time and reminds you that, yes, there was at least one bright spot in the day.

Another low-pressure option is *The Three Good Things Tactic.* As you're winding down, mentally list three things from your day that went well. They don't have to be life-changing—maybe your coffee was extra good, you got through a meeting without technical issues, or your dog didn't bark during your entire work call. By focusing on these small positives, you're helping your brain shift from the day's stresses to the day's wins. It's like a quick recap of all the little victories you may have overlooked.

For a fun twist, try *The Gratitude Jar (or Box, or Shoe, Whatever You Have).* Keep a small container by your bed and whenever something good happens, jot it down on a piece of paper and toss it in. It could be a compliment someone gave you, a goal you reached, or even a good hair day. You don't have to write something every day—just whenever something memorable happens. Over time, you'll have a collection of positive moments to look back on. And let's face it, on a rough day, pulling out a few of those notes can be a quick reminder that good things do happen.

If you're sharing a bed with a partner, try *The One Thing Exchange.* Before going to sleep, each of you shares one thing you're grateful for. It's a nice way to connect, and hearing someone else's gratitude can bring a fresh perspective to your own day. You might find yourself appreciating the little things more, and it's a lighthearted, positive way to wrap up the day together. Plus, it's way more interesting than the classic "How was your day?" exchange.

Another super-easy approach is *The "Thank You" Reflection.* This one's a bit more abstract but equally calming. As you settle into bed, think of someone or something in your life you'd like to thank mentally. Maybe it's a friend who's been supportive, your pet who gives you endless affection, or even just the cozy bed you're lying in. This quiet mental "thank you" doesn't require anything written down, but it leaves you with a sense of peace and appreciation that helps ease you into sleep.

And for those who love a tech twist, there's *The Photo Scroll of Gratitude.* Open up your camera roll and scroll through a few recent photos that make you smile. Maybe it's a picture of a meal you loved, a funny moment you captured, or a friend's selfie. This visual approach to gratitude is simple and surprisingly uplifting. Looking back at happy moments from recent days can remind you of the good times, giving your evening a gentle positivity boost.

With these no-stress gratitude techniques, you can end your day on a positive note without feeling like you're taking on a project. A small gratitude practice helps you shift focus from worries to wins, bringing a little more calm and contentment to your bedtime routine.

Creating a Peaceful Environment with Simple Bedtime Habits

There's nothing like a peaceful, cozy environment to help ease you into sleep. Unfortunately, the bedroom can often feel more like a storage closet or tech station than a relaxing oasis. But with a few simple tweaks, you can turn your space into a calm, restful retreat. No major renovations needed—just a few small changes that make winding down feel like something you actually look forward to.

First up is *The "Clear the Clutter" Quick Fix.* You don't need a spotless room, but clearing away a bit of clutter can work wonders for your peace of mind. A quick tidying session—putting away that pile of clothes or organizing the nightstand—can make the room feel a little less chaotic. Think of it as creating a clean slate for sleep. And if all else fails, tossing everything into a closet or drawer for the night is always an option. Out of sight, out of mind, right?

Next, bring in *The Soft Lighting Trick.* Swap out bright overhead lights for a softer bedside lamp or even a few candles (battery-powered ones work if you're worried about falling asleep mid-relax). This dim lighting helps signal to your brain that it's time to wind down. It's a subtle but powerful way to set the mood for relaxation, plus it feels way cozier than blasting fluorescent light around the room. Think "spa vibes" instead of "interrogation room."

For an extra touch of calm, try *The Pillow Fluff and Blanket Fold.* Taking a few seconds to arrange your pillows and fold back the blanket can make your bed look more inviting. It sounds silly, but it's amazing how a neatly made bed can make you feel like you're stepping into a luxury hotel. You're not just going to bed; you're entering a sleep sanctuary where you're the VIP guest. Throw in an extra fluffy pillow or two, and suddenly, your bed feels like a cloud waiting to catch you.

To create a peaceful sensory experience, try adding *A Soothing Scent.* A quick spritz of lavender spray on your pillow or a few drops of essential oil near the bed can instantly add a calming vibe to your room. Lavender, chamomile, or eucalyptus are great choices, but even the scent of a favorite lotion can work. It's like adding an invisible layer of calm to the room, making your space feel less like an ordinary bedroom and more like a relaxation retreat.

Another trick to add to your routine is *The Tech Timeout.* If you're used to scrolling or watching TV right up until bed, try putting the screens away about 30 minutes before you hit the pillow. Blue light from screens can mess with your melatonin levels, making it harder to fall asleep. Instead, swap the phone for a book, a journal, or even a bit of quiet music. It's not about giving up screens forever—just giving yourself a break before bed. Trust me, the internet will still be there tomorrow.

For a little extra comfort, consider adding *The Cozy Socks or Blanket Touch*. Cold feet can actually make it harder to fall asleep, so slipping on a pair of soft socks or cozying up with an extra blanket can make a surprising difference. Plus, who doesn't feel 10% more relaxed when wrapped in something soft and warm? It's like a personal little cocoon, adding an extra layer of coziness to your evening routine.

Finally, wind down with *The Breathing Break*. Just before you close your eyes, take a few deep breaths—inhale slowly, hold, and exhale gently. This mini-breathing exercise helps you release any lingering tension from the day. Think of it as a mental "power off" button for your brain. After all, you deserve a full recharge, and taking a few seconds to unwind can help set the stage for better sleep.

With these small but effective bedtime habits, creating a peaceful environment becomes easy and enjoyable. Each little step invites you into a calm, cozy space where sleep can come naturally. Your bedroom might not be a luxury retreat, but with these tweaks, it'll feel pretty close.

Breathing Techniques for a Calm Mind and Restful Sleep

Nothing says "I'm ready for sleep," quite like staring at the ceiling while your mind plays a highlight reel of every awkward thing you've ever done. But a few well-chosen breathing techniques can help quiet the mental chatter, signaling to your brain that it's time to knock off for the night. Breathing exercises might sound too simple to work, but they're surprisingly effective—and no special skills or yoga pants required.

First, there's *The 4-7-8 Technique*. This one's a favorite for a reason. Start by breathing in through your nose for a count of 4, hold your breath for a count of 7 (yes, you can do it), and then exhale through your mouth for a count of 8, as if you're blowing out a thousand birthday candles. Repeat this a few times. It's like telling your brain, "We're done here. Time to power down." With each round, you'll feel your heartbeat slow, and your body relax. If you're lucky, you'll be asleep by the time you reach the fourth round, and your brain won't know what hit it.

Then there's *Box Breathing,* also known as square breathing. Imagine a square in your mind. Breathe in for a count of 4 as you mentally trace the first side, hold for 4 on the second side, exhale for 4 on the third, and hold again for 4 on the fourth. It's basically an adult version of drawing with crayons but with breathing. This technique is perfect for quieting a busy brain that's in overdrive, gently telling it, "Hey, it's bedtime, not 'let's overanalyze everything' time." By focusing on the square, you're giving your brain a mental timeout.

For the math-inclined, there's *The Counting Breath.* Simply breathe in, and as you exhale, count "one." Next, exhale, count "two." Keep going up to ten, then start over. It sounds basic, but the counting is just enough to distract your mind from racing thoughts. If your brain tries to sneak in a reminder about that embarrassing moment from 2009, kindly tell it you're busy counting. You might find that by the time you hit ten, you're already halfway to dreamland.

Then there's *The Diaphragmatic Breath,* also known as "belly breathing," which sounds much fancier than it is. Place one hand on your belly and the other on your chest, and breathe in deeply through your nose, letting your belly rise. Exhale slowly, feeling it fall. It's like giving your body a gentle, rhythmic hug. The belly-breathing technique helps signal the body to calm down, like pressing "snooze" on your own stress. It's simple but surprisingly soothing, and if nothing else, it gives you something calming to focus on that isn't tomorrow's to-do list.

For a little extra pizzazz, try *The Wave Breath*. Picture each inhale as a gentle wave coming up to the shore and each exhale as the wave returning to the sea. Visualize this rhythm as you breathe, letting the "waves" lull you into a peaceful state. No beach needed—just imagine yourself as a human ocean with a steady, calming tide. It's surprisingly relaxing, and you might find yourself snoozing right on that imaginary beach.

Finally, there's *The Sighing Exhale*. Take a deep breath, then let it out with a big, exaggerated sigh. Go ahead, let it be loud. It's like telling your body, "I'm officially done with this day." Repeat a few times and let the tension melt away. Not only does this cue your nervous system to chill, but there's something oddly satisfying about sighing dramatically. Bonus points if your sighing actually makes you chuckle at yourself—by then, you'll be so relaxed you might drift right off.

These breathing exercises might seem simple, but that's their charm. They're quick, easy, and perfect for silencing a busy brain that insists on reliving the day's dramas. The next time you're staring at the ceiling, give one of these techniques a try and see if you can breathe your way to sleep. You might just find that a good night's rest is only a few breaths away.

A good night's sleep doesn't have to be as elusive as it seems. With a few simple routines, like clearing clutter, practicing gratitude, setting a calming environment, and adding a bit of deep breathing, bedtime can transform from a restless struggle into a truly relaxing experience. These small wind-down rituals bring a touch of calm to the end of your day, helping you drift off with less stress and more peace. Now that you've mastered the art of unwinding, it's time to embrace self-care from another angle. In the next chapter, we'll explore how embracing imperfections in your self-care journey can be just as important as the routines themselves. After all, self-care doesn't have to be "perfect" to be effective.

EIGHT

Embracing Imperfection: When Self-Care Isn't "Perfect" (and That's Okay)

Self-care often gets painted as this serene, Instagram-worthy experience—perfectly folded blankets, flawlessly brewed tea, and journal entries in the world's best handwriting. But real life is messy, and so is self-care. In this chapter, we'll dive into why self-care doesn't have to be perfect to be beneficial. Whether you're laughing at a self-care "fail" or celebrating the tiny steps you're managing, embracing imperfection can be its own form of self-care. Because sometimes, a half-done yoga routine or a microwaved "gourmet" meal is as good as it gets—and that's absolutely okay.

Learning to Laugh at Self-Care Attempts That Don't Go as Planned

If there's one thing self-care can teach us, it's that sometimes, things just don't go as planned—and that's okay. We've all had those moments: the "relaxing" bubble bath that turns cold before you've had a chance to unwind, the "mindful" meditation interrupted by a barking dog, or the attempt at yoga that ends with a tangled mat and a bruised ego. The truth is, self-care isn't about perfection; it's about trying, adjusting, and, yes, sometimes laughing at how hilariously wrong it can go.

One classic example? *The At-Home Spa Day Fail.* You've got the face mask, the cucumber slices, and maybe even some "soothing" music playing in the background. But just as you settle in, the doorbell rings, the face mask feels like it's glued to your skin, and the cucumbers end up in your mouth instead of on your eyes. It's in these moments that the best approach is to laugh it off. Self-care isn't ruined because of a few hiccups—in fact, the chaos might even be the most relaxing part if you let yourself see the humor in it.

Then there's *The DIY Aromatherapy Disaster.* Essential oils are supposed to be calming, right? But if you've ever spilled a bottle of lavender oil on your carpet or accidentally diffused a scent that smelled suspiciously like cough medicine, you know the struggle. Instead of the serene, spa-like atmosphere you pictured, you end up with a room that smells like a dentist's office. It's not exactly the zen vibe you were going for, but hey, at least your space smells... memorable? The key is to laugh it off and try again (maybe with a smaller drop next time).

And we can't forget *The Perfectly Planned Morning Routine Meltdown.* Maybe you set your alarm early, laid out your workout clothes, and planned a beautiful, mindful start to your day. But then the snooze button happens. Before you know it, the "morning routine" has turned into a mad dash to get dressed, coffee spilling, and a mental promise to "try again tomorrow." The irony is that self-care was supposed to be about reducing stress, not racing against the clock. Sometimes, the best self-care in these moments is just a chuckle at the whole fiasco and a reminder that it's okay to be human.

Of course, there's also *The Mindful Cooking Mishap.* Picture this: you're following a recipe for a nourishing, home-cooked meal. You've got your ingredients prepped, you're feeling calm... and then you realize you forgot to set the timer. What was supposed to be a "lightly roasted" dinner is now a crispy surprise. While it's tempting to declare the whole meal (and self-care attempt) a disaster, try to see the humor in your charred masterpiece. Even the most experienced chefs have "creative outcomes," and nobody said self-care had to taste good.

If you've ever tried *Meditation with Pets Around,* you know the struggle. Just as you're about to reach a peaceful state, your pet decides this is the perfect moment for attention. Maybe your cat saunters across your lap, or your dog insists that your "zen space" is actually a play zone. It's impossible to focus, but that's okay. Sometimes, self-care means rolling with the unexpected—like a surprise cuddle session in the middle of meditation. After all, who needs absolute silence when you've got a pet by your side?

The truth is, self-care doesn't have to be flawless to work. Sometimes, the best moments come from the laughter and flexibility that happen when things go wrong. Embracing these "fails" as part of the process takes the pressure off. So, the next time your carefully planned self-care routine doesn't go as expected, let yourself laugh it off and enjoy the imperfection. Self-care is about taking care of yourself—messy, real, and perfectly imperfect.

Stories of Funny Self-Care "Fails" to Normalize Imperfection

Self-care is supposed to be calming, rejuvenating, and uplifting. But anyone who's tried to pull off a Pinterest-worthy self-care routine knows it doesn't always go that way. From failed yoga poses to catastrophic face masks, self-care "fails" are more common than we like to admit. Embracing these blunders as part of the journey can be its own form of therapy—because nothing feels better than a good laugh at ourselves.

One popular self-care "fail" is *The Yoga Pose That Went Wrong*. You see a picture of a graceful yoga pose and think, "I could totally do that." Fast forward to you on the living room floor, half-bent and trying to remember how to breathe while wondering why your leg won't go where it's supposed to. Instead of reaching a state of zen, you're left wondering if you'll ever walk straight again. The best part? That accidental tangle of limbs becomes a memory that makes you laugh every time. Yoga may be about finding inner peace, but sometimes, finding humor in failed poses is the real reward.

Then there's *The "Calm Bath" Catastrophe*. You've got the candles, the bath bomb, and your favorite relaxing playlist. But within minutes, the water's lukewarm, the bath bomb's turned the water a suspicious shade of green, and there's so much steam that you feel like you're in a swamp rather than a spa. Not to mention the bubbles, which somehow overflowed and are now creeping ominously towards the bathroom floor. What was supposed to be your ultimate relaxation time has somehow become a mini stress-fest. But hey, at least your bathroom now looks like a scene from a soap opera—literally.

And then, of course, there's *The DIY Face Mask Disaster*. Armed with honey, yogurt, or maybe some mashed avocado, you whip up a "natural" face mask. It's supposed to give you glowing skin, but instead, it feels like sticky cement. Ten minutes later, you're trying to wash it off, only to find that half of it is glued to your face, and the other half is clogging the sink. Suddenly, you're covered in more mask than you started with, and instead of looking radiant, you look like a kid who lost a food fight. The moral? Some things are best left to the professionals—or, at the very least, to products that don't belong in your fridge.

Of course, we can't skip *The Meditation Meltdown*. You've found the perfect spot, closed your eyes, and taken a deep breath, ready for inner peace. Five seconds later, you remember that thing you forgot to do. Two minutes in, your nose itches, and three minutes in, you're thinking about snacks. By the end of the session, you've mentally reorganized your pantry and still can't remember if you were supposed to inhale or exhale. But the good news? Meditation doesn't have to be perfect, and the mere attempt is progress. Sometimes, a half-done meditation session is still better than no meditation at all.

Then there's *The Cozy Blanket Trap.* You've got the fluffiest blanket, a great book, and a warm drink. Everything's perfect—until you realize that the blanket has swallowed you whole, your drink is just out of reach, and you're far too cozy to even attempt getting up. Your quest for ultimate coziness has left you a blanket prisoner stuck in your own "comfort zone." This is the kind of self-care fail we can all laugh at—who knew relaxation could be so much work?

Finally, there's *The "No-Tech" Challenge,* where you vow to put away all devices for an evening. Fifteen minutes in, you've cleaned the kitchen, organized your shoes, and suddenly realize that silence is, well, kind of loud. By the end of the hour, you're sneaking glances at your phone like it's a forbidden fruit. Sometimes, the "unplugged" life isn't as easy as it looks, and that's okay. The fact that you tried at all is worth a pat on the back.

These self-care "fails" remind us that it's okay to laugh when things don't go as planned. Embracing the imperfection in self-care makes the process all the more real—and a lot more fun. Self-care isn't about flawless routines; it's about doing something for yourself, however messy it might look.

Letting Go of the Pressure to Do Self-Care "Right"

Somewhere along the way, self-care started to feel like a competition. With social media full of serene self-care posts—perfectly arranged candles, spotless yoga mats, and that ever-elusive "glow"—it's easy to feel like you're doing it all wrong if your version of self-care doesn't look like a magazine cover. But the truth is, there's no "right" way to do self-care. In fact, letting go of the pressure to do it perfectly can be one of the most freeing things you can do for yourself.

Consider *The Ideal Morning Routine Pressure.* You know the one: waking up early, meditating, journaling, drinking a green smoothie, and getting a workout in—all before sunrise. It sounds amazing... in theory. But in reality? Some days you hit snooze, skip the workout and opt for coffee over kale. And that's okay! The idea isn't to live up to an impossible standard; it's to give yourself what you need, even if that means an extra hour of sleep or a slower morning. You don't get extra points for perfection; in fact, self-care is more about finding balance than following a strict list.

Then there's *The All-or-Nothing Trap.* Often, it feels like self-care is only "worth it" if you go all out. If you can't do the full face mask, bath soak, and spa-level pampering session, why bother, right? Wrong. Self-care doesn't have to be a grand gesture. Taking five minutes to breathe, sitting quietly with a cup of tea, or listening to a favorite song can be just as restorative as a full-blown spa day. It's not about doing it all; it's about doing what you can when you can. In fact, some of the best self-care moments are the tiny ones you barely notice, like stretching for two minutes or taking a quick walk outside.

One of the biggest pressures in self-care is *The "Perfect Space" Myth.* We're led to believe that self-care only counts if you have the ideal setting—dim lighting, expensive candles, and a flawless, clutter-free room. But here's the reality: self-care can happen anywhere, even if you're sitting on a couch next to a pile of unfolded laundry. You don't need a five-star spa setup to unwind. Sometimes, the most effective self-care happens in the middle of real life, not in a staged photo-op. Embracing your surroundings, no matter how chaotic, can be self-care in itself.

Let's not forget *The Comparison Game.* It's easy to look around and feel like everyone else is "better" at self-care. Maybe your friend is into hot yoga, or your coworker is posting about their meditation retreat. But self-care isn't a one-size-fits-all. Just because someone else finds peace in ways that look impressive doesn't mean that your routine is any less valuable. Maybe your version of self-care is taking time to bake or reading a few pages of a novel. Self-care is personal, and what works for someone else doesn't have to be your path. The only comparison worth making is to how you felt before and after your own routine.

Finally, there's *The "Should" Syndrome*. This is the feeling that self-care only "counts" if it's productive. We tend to think we should be journaling, meditating, and reflecting deeply every time. But self-care isn't about ticking boxes—it's about doing what makes you feel good. If binge-watching your favorite show, doing a puzzle, or baking a batch of cookies is what relaxes you, then that's self-care! Giving yourself permission to do what actually feels right, instead of what you "should" do, is a huge part of letting go of self-care pressure.

Self-care is about taking care of yourself, not impressing anyone else or following a perfect formula. Letting go of the pressure to do it "right" is freeing. It means embracing what works for you in whatever way fits your life. After all, the only self-care worth practicing is the kind that actually leaves you feeling refreshed, no matter how it looks from the outside.

Celebrating Small Victories and Progress, Even if It's Minimal

Self-care isn't about conquering mountains; it's about the tiny hills you climb every day—like drinking actual water, putting your phone down for ten minutes, or eating something other than cereal for dinner. In the world of self-care, small wins deserve a party. These little victories make life feel just a bit better, and they're definitely worth celebrating, even if you're the only one cheering yourself on.

First, there's *The Hydration Triumph.* We've all been told to drink more water, yet somehow it feels like an Olympic event. So, if you manage to down a whole glass, pat yourself on the back. Forget fancy hydration apps; just finishing that glass without getting distracted is enough. It's a quiet victory but a real one. Hydration may be the underdog of self-care, but when you take that last sip, you're basically a health icon.

Then there's *The Bedtime Routine Accomplishment.* You brushed your teeth, put on pajamas, and didn't end up watching videos in bed for an hour? You've hit the self-care jackpot! Establishing any kind of bedtime routine—no matter how minimal—is a win. It doesn't need to be perfect. Just turning off the lights and actually lying down without first googling "random facts" is an achievement worthy of applause. Give yourself some credit for not waking up with your phone still in your hand.

Another win to celebrate is *The Kitchen Creation.* You managed to cook? Even if it's just reheating leftovers or whipping up a sandwich, congratulations! The bar doesn't have to be high. If you resisted the urge to order takeout and made something edible, you're winning at life. Sure, the "meal" might be toast and scrambled eggs, but it's a solid victory. Self-care isn't about Michelin stars; it's about not burning down the kitchen. And if your cooking actually tasted good? You might as well give yourself a chef's hat.

Then there's *The Outdoors Adventure.* Did you leave the house today? Maybe it was just a quick walk around the block or stepping outside to check the weather, but fresh air is fresh air. Whether it's a five-minute stroll or just breathing deeply on your balcony, any encounter with the great outdoors counts as self-care. This is basically you channeling your inner nature lover—okay, maybe not quite, but at least you got some vitamin D. No need for a long hike; just showing up outside is worth celebrating.

Next up is *The Tiny Tidy-Up*. Cleaning is one of those self-care activities that we think has to be a big event. But tidying up one corner or putting away some stray socks? That's real progress. Even organizing the junk drawer for five minutes deserves a medal in the self-care Olympics. You don't need a spotless house to feel like a domestic genius. It's the little steps that make your space a bit more livable—and let's be real, your future self will thank you when you're not tripping over yesterday's socks.

And don't forget *The Social Contact Achievement*. Maybe you sent a funny meme to a friend, responded to a message, or actually called your mom back. Social interaction is exhausting, so any effort at all is worthy of a celebration. Reaching out, even briefly, counts as self-care. Sometimes, self-care is just saying, "Hey, I'm alive!" to someone in your contacts list. It's low-stakes, high-impact, and a reminder that you're maintaining connections one text at a time.

In the self-care journey, small victories are the unsung heroes. Hydrating, tidying, or even cooking toast—it all adds up. These little moments don't require fanfare, but they're still worth a pat on the back. By celebrating your tiny achievements, you're building a practice that's rooted in kindness to yourself, one glass of water and one folded sock at a time.

Self-care doesn't have to look like a flawless spa day to be meaningful. From laughing at our self-care "fails" to celebrating the little victories (hello, drinking a glass of water!), embracing imperfection is key to building a self-care routine that feels real and sustainable. These small, sometimes messy moments are what make self-care truly personal. Now that we've explored the joys of imperfect self-care, it's time to turn inward. In the next chapter, we'll dive into the art of self-compassion—how to practice kindness toward yourself and let go of self-criticism. Get ready to be your own best friend.

NINE

Self-Compassion as a Form of Self-Care

You've probably heard the saying, "You're your own worst critic," but some days it feels more like you're your own personal heckler, sitting in the cheap seats and shouting things like, "Nice move, genius!" But here's the thing: being hard on yourself isn't helping. What if, instead of roasting yourself like a bad stand-up routine, you started cheering yourself on? Self-compassion is about treating yourself with the same kindness and understanding you'd show a good friend—or at least a decent acquaintance. In this chapter, we'll dive into how giving yourself a break (literally and figuratively) can transform your self-care game. Spoiler alert: you'll feel way better when you stop being your own worst frenemy.

Practicing Self-Kindness Through Difficult Moments

We've all had those days. You spill coffee on your shirt, forget the one thing you meant to remember, and stub your toe just to top it off. The inner critic comes alive with a vengeance, ready to remind you how "useless" or "clumsy" you are. But here's the deal: beating yourself up doesn't make the coffee spill less sticky, and it certainly doesn't make you feel any better. This is where self-kindness comes in —your ultimate superpower for turning tough moments into something a little less terrible.

First, let's acknowledge the obvious: being kind to yourself doesn't come naturally to most people. We're so used to showing compassion to others that when it comes to ourselves, we default to tough love. But tough love is just a fancy term for being unnecessarily harsh. Imagine if your best friend spilled coffee on their shirt and you said, "Wow, could you be any worse at drinking beverages?" Exactly— you'd never say that (and if you would, maybe rethink your friendship style). So why talk to yourself that way?

When life gets messy, one of the best things you can do is practice *The Pause and Reframe.* Pause when things go wrong, take a deep breath, and reframe how you're talking to yourself. Instead of "I can't believe I messed this up again," try "It's okay, I'll figure it out." This doesn't mean sugarcoating reality—it's just about treating yourself with a little gentleness. It's like wrapping a mistake in bubble wrap: it's still there, but at least it's cushioned.

Another trick is embracing *The "What Would You Say to a Friend?" Test.* Imagine a friend called you in tears over the same problem you're dealing with. What would you say to them? Chances are, it wouldn't be, "You're the absolute worst, and you should feel bad about it." Instead, you'd probably say something supportive, like, "It's not a big deal, and you'll get through this." Now, take those words and say them to yourself. Sure, it might feel a little weird at first, but your brain will thank you for not turning on itself.

And then there's *The Permission to Be Human Rule.* We all have moments when we drop the ball—or the entire box of metaphorical oranges. That's life. Giving yourself permission to make mistakes doesn't mean you're slacking; it means you're acknowledging that perfection is impossible. So, you forgot to reply to an email or burned dinner for the third time this week? Guess what? You're human. Let yourself off the hook with a simple phrase like, "Whoops, that happened," and move on.

One of the sneakiest ways to be kind to yourself is through *The Self-Care Countermove.* When things go wrong, our first instinct is often to spiral—obsess over the mistake, replay it in our minds, and dwell on all the ways we could have done better. Instead, try a counterintuitive approach: do something nice for yourself. Whether it's a hot cup of tea, a quick walk, or a five-minute dance break to your favorite song, these small acts of self-care remind you that you deserve kindness, especially when you're feeling down.

The truth is, self-kindness isn't about pretending everything is fine. It's about showing yourself the same understanding you'd offer anyone else who's having a tough day. It's about pausing before you pile on the guilt and saying, "Hey, it's okay to have an off moment." By practicing self-kindness, you're building a habit of resilience—one that makes even the worst days feel a little more manageable. And if all else fails, remember this: nobody's perfect, and that's what makes life so wonderfully unpredictable.

Exercises for Building a Gentler Inner Voice and Letting Go of Guilt

Let's face it—your inner voice can sometimes be a bit of a jerk. It's that running commentary that pipes up at the worst times, saying things like, "Wow, that was dumb," or "Why can't you get it together?" But here's the good news: with a little practice, you can turn your inner critic into something much more supportive—like a cheerleader with slightly less glitter. It's all about training that voice to be gentler, kinder, and far less judgy.

Start with *The Compliment Rewind.* Think back to something kind someone said to you recently—maybe a coworker complimented your work, or a friend said you're a great listener. Now, take that compliment and repeat it to yourself, out loud if possible. It might feel awkward at first, but hearing kind words, even if they're coming from your own mouth, helps rewire your brain to focus on the positive. Bonus points if you add, "And I totally deserve this compliment" at the end. Because you do.

Next, there's *The "Dear Best Friend" Letter*. When you're being especially hard on yourself, write down what you'd say to your best friend in the same situation. It could be something as simple as "You're doing your best, and that's enough," or as enthusiastic as, "You're an incredible human, and one mistake doesn't define you!" Now read the letter back to yourself, but replace their name with your own. This exercise isn't just sweet—it's an instant reminder that you're worthy of the same kindness you show others.

If you want to take things to the next level, try *The Daily Self-Compliment Challenge*. Every day, think of one thing you did well and say it out loud to yourself. It could be as big as finishing a major project or as small as remembering to water the plants. No achievement is too minor to celebrate. The trick is to make this a habit so your brain gets used to hearing positive reinforcement. Over time, your inner critic will start to lose its edge, replaced by a voice that's more like, "Hey, look at you go!"

For those guilt-ridden moments, *The "It's Okay" Mantra* works wonders. When you catch yourself feeling guilty for something small —like forgetting a birthday or eating the last slice of cake—pause and say, "It's okay." That's it. No overanalyzing, no beating yourself up. Just a simple acknowledgment that mistakes and indulgences are part of being human. If you need to get fancy, you can add a follow-up, like, "It's okay—I'll do better next time," or, "It's okay—cake is delicious." The point is to let go of the guilt and move forward.

Another great exercise is *The Gratitude Mirror*. Stand in front of a mirror and name three things you're grateful for about yourself. They don't have to be groundbreaking—maybe you love your sense of humor, or you're proud of how you handled a tough situation. If you feel like you're bragging, good! This is your time to hype yourself up. The mirror doesn't judge—it just reflects back a person who deserves kindness.

Finally, there's *The Self-Kindness Jar.* Find an empty jar (or a box, or even a shoe—it's flexible), and every time you catch yourself being kind to yourself, write it down and toss it in. Maybe you said no to an extra work project, took a break when you were overwhelmed or forgave yourself for a mistake. Watching the jar fill up over time is a tangible reminder of all the ways you're learning to treat yourself better. Plus, it's a lot harder to argue with a jar full of evidence.

Building a gentler inner voice takes time, but these exercises are a great start. Each little act of self-kindness chips away at that inner critic, making room for a voice that's supportive, understanding, and even a little bit proud of you. And let's be honest—your brain deserves a cheerleader way more than it deserves a heckler.

Encouragement to Acknowledge Your Efforts with Compassion

How often do you take a moment to actually acknowledge the effort you put into life? Probably not enough. Most of us are pros at spotting where we "fell short" but less skilled at giving ourselves credit for what we managed to pull off—especially when we're juggling 800 things at once. It's time to flip that script and start seeing your daily efforts for what they are: proof that you're doing your best, even if it doesn't always feel like it.

Think about it: you got out of bed today. Maybe you even brushed your teeth or put on pants. That's effort. Did you eat something resembling a meal? Extra points! These small, everyday tasks are easy to overlook, but they're evidence that you're showing up for life— even on days when it feels like life is showing up for *you.* Start giving yourself credit for these victories, no matter how tiny they seem. Brushed your hair? Amazing. Remembered to charge your phone? Incredible. Survived a Zoom meeting with your camera on? Heroic.

Acknowledging your efforts isn't just about celebrating the little things—it's also about recognizing the emotional work you do. For instance, maybe you comforted a friend who was having a rough day, kept your cool when someone cut you off in traffic or resisted the urge to say something snarky in a group chat. These aren't tasks you can check off a to-do list, but they take energy, and that deserves acknowledgment. Being a decent human is no small feat, especially when the world feels like a reality TV show with no off button.

One way to practice this is through *The "What Did I Do Today?" Check-In*. At the end of the day, take five minutes to mentally list what you accomplished, no matter how small. Maybe you answered a couple of emails, remembered to pay a bill, or managed to find socks that matched. These might not seem like groundbreaking achievements, but they're part of keeping life moving forward. By focusing on what you *did* instead of what you didn't, you're retraining your brain to see your effort as valuable—even when it's not flashy.

For a more creative approach, try *The Celebration Jar*. Every time you do something worth celebrating, jot it down on a piece of paper and toss it in. It could be something simple, like cleaning the kitchen, or something big, like getting through a tough conversation. Over time, the jar will fill up with proof of your hard work. On days when you feel like you're not doing enough, pull out a few notes and remind yourself of all the things you've achieved. It's like a greatest-hits album of your life, except you're the only artist on the tracklist.

Another technique is *The 3-for-1 Compliment Rule*. For every one thing you criticize yourself for, find three things you did well. Example: "I forgot to reply to that email" gets balanced with "But I remembered to call my mom, I crushed that presentation, and I didn't burn dinner." This isn't about ignoring mistakes—it's about giving yourself a more balanced view. After all, you're not just your flaws; you're also your strengths, and those deserve just as much airtime.

Lastly, consider *The Lazy Day Hall Pass*. Some days, the only effort you manage is staying alive, and guess what? That counts. Let yourself acknowledge that even doing the bare minimum is still effort. Surviving is hard work sometimes, and you deserve a round of applause for making it through the day, even if all you did was watch TV in your pajamas. Self-compassion isn't just for your "productive" days—it's for all of them.

By taking the time to acknowledge your efforts, you're building a habit of compassion that can transform how you see yourself. You're not lazy, unproductive, or falling short—you're a human being, doing your best in a complicated world. So, give yourself a pat on the back, a gold star, or even just a deep breath. You've earned it.

Creating a Self-Compassion Mantra for Daily Use

Mantras are like little pep talks you can give yourself without needing a motivational speaker or a crowd cheering you on. The best part? They're portable, customizable, and always available—kind of like a pocket-sized life coach that doesn't charge by the hour. When it comes to self-compassion, a mantra can be your go-to tool for those moments when your inner critic starts throwing shade or when life feels like it's doing its best to trip you up.

Creating a mantra doesn't mean you have to get overly spiritual or start chanting in Sanskrit (unless that's your thing, in which case, go for it!). A self-compassion mantra can be as simple as a sentence or phrase that reminds you to be kind to yourself. Think of it as a verbal reset button—a quick reminder that you're doing your best, even when things aren't going perfectly.

Start with *The Keep-It-Simple Approach*. A good mantra doesn't have to be Shakespearean—it just needs to resonate with you. Something like "I'm doing my best, and that's enough" or "Mistakes are part of learning" works wonders. If you prefer a bit of humor, try "Progress, not perfection" or "At least I tried, which is more than some people can say." The key is finding something that feels authentic to you, not something that sounds like it belongs on a motivational poster.

For those extra-tough days, you might need *The Emergency Mantra*. This is the one you pull out when things are truly falling apart—like when you've locked your keys in the car, spilled coffee on your shirt, and realized you forgot your wallet all in the same morning. In those moments, a mantra like "This too shall pass" or "I'll laugh about this later" can help you survive the chaos with a little more grace (and maybe even a chuckle).

Another fun option is *The Personal Touch Mantra*. Customize your mantra with something specific to you. For example, if you're always pushing yourself too hard, you could go with "I deserve rest." If you tend to overthink, try "It's okay to let this go." The more tailored your mantra is to your personality and challenges, the more powerful it will be. Bonus points if it makes you smile when you say it.

Once you've chosen your mantra, make it a habit to use it daily. Say it to yourself in the mirror, write it on a sticky note and stick it on your desk, or set it as your phone wallpaper. The more you see and repeat your mantra, the more it will become a natural part of your thought process. Over time, it will start to replace those automatic negative thoughts with something kinder and more supportive. Think of it as your brain's new ringtone—less "critical overload" and more "gentle encouragement."

The beauty of a self-compassion mantra is that it's always there when you need it. Whether you're dealing with a tough day, a frustrating mistake, or just the general chaos of life, having a simple, kind phrase to lean on can make all the difference. It's like having your own mini cheer squad in your pocket, reminding you that you're enough, you're trying, and that's more than okay.

Self-compassion is a practice, not a destination, and your mantra is one small but mighty way to keep that practice alive. So, take a moment to create one that speaks to you—and don't be afraid to adjust it over time. Your mantra is there to serve you, not the other way around. And remember, the fact that you're even trying to be kinder to yourself is a huge step in the right direction.

As we move forward, we'll explore how these moments of self-compassion can help us tackle stress in its many sneaky forms. In the next chapter, we'll dive into quick, effective ways to manage stress in five minutes or less—because, let's be honest, we all need a shortcut sometimes.

TEN

Managing Stress in 5 Minutes or Less

Stress is like that overly enthusiastic coworker who never takes a break—it shows up uninvited, dominates your mental space, and always seems to catch you at the worst times. Luckily, you don't need an hour-long yoga session or a luxury retreat to tackle it. Sometimes, all you need is five minutes and a good strategy to keep stress from turning your brain into a chaotic hamster wheel. In this chapter, we'll explore quick, effective stress-busting techniques that you can use anytime, anywhere. They're simple and fast and might even make that hamster wheel a little less wobbly.

Grounding Techniques for Calming Nerves in High-Stress Moments

Stress has a way of sneaking up on you like a stealthy ninja—one minute, you're fine, and the next, you're spiraling into a vortex of "what ifs." The good news? You don't have to let stress take over. Grounding techniques are quick, effective ways to bring you back to the present and keep your nerves from running the show. Think of them as your emergency brakes for when life feels like it's speeding out of control.

One of the simplest grounding tricks is *The 5-4-3-2-1 Method.* When your mind is racing faster than a toddler on a sugar high, this exercise can help you reconnect with the present. Start by naming five things you can see around you (bonus points if you find something weird, like a plant that's clearly seen better days). Then, identify four things you can touch, three things you can hear, two things you can smell (or wish you couldn't), and one thing you can taste. By the time you've worked your way through the list, your brain has shifted focus, and the stress ninja is suddenly less intimidating.

Another favorite is *The Barefoot Trick.* If you're at home or somewhere it won't raise eyebrows, take off your shoes and let your feet touch the ground. Focus on the feeling of the floor beneath you —its texture, temperature, or even how oddly comforting it is to have your toes free. It's a small gesture, but it helps ground you (literally and figuratively) and reminds you that you're supported, even when life feels unsteady.

For those who prefer movement, try *The Wiggle and Shake.* Stand up and start shaking out your hands, arms, and legs. Wiggle your shoulders, give your head a gentle shake, and maybe even bounce on your toes. This quick burst of movement releases pent-up tension and gets your body on the same page as your mind. Plus, it's impossible to take yourself too seriously when you're wiggling like a cartoon character. By the time you stop, you'll feel lighter—mentally and physically.

If you're feeling overwhelmed, *The Anchor Phrase* is a lifesaver. Choose a short, calming phrase that resonates with you, like "I'm safe," "This will pass," or "I can handle this." When stress strikes, repeat your phrase out loud or in your head until it feels like a mantra. It's like having a personal cheerleader, except you don't have to explain yourself to an actual human. The repetition grounds you, reminding you that you're in control—even if your brain is trying to convince you otherwise.

One grounding technique that's great for public spaces is *The Sensory Object.* Carry a small item with you—a smooth stone, a coin, or even a paperclip—and use it as a touchpoint when stress kicks in. Focus on its texture, weight, and temperature, letting it bring you back to the present moment. Bonus points if it's something unique enough to spark a bit of curiosity, like a lucky charm or a tiny figurine. By redirecting your attention to this object, you're giving your brain a chance to reset.

Lastly, there's *The Breathe-and-Sigh Combo.* Inhale deeply through your nose, hold it for a second, and then exhale with an audible sigh —yes, a big, dramatic one. Not only does this physically release tension, but it also sends a signal to your nervous system to calm down. Repeat a few times, and you'll feel your body and mind start to sync up in a way that says, "Okay, maybe we've got this after all."

Stress might be sneaky, but with these grounding techniques, you've got a toolbox full of ways to handle it. They're quick, subtle (well, maybe not the wiggling), and perfect for tackling those high-stress moments that seem to pop up out of nowhere. The next time stress tries to take over, ground yourself, take a deep breath, and remind that ninja who's boss.

Physical Relaxation Exercises to Quickly Release Tension

Stress has a funny way of taking up residence in our bodies— sneaking into our shoulders, knotting up our backs, or making us clench our jaws like we're auditioning for a role as a human nutcracker. Luckily, you don't need a personal masseuse or an hour-long yoga class to release tension. These quick physical relaxation exercises are simple, effective, and can be done almost anywhere—yes, even at your desk.

Let's start with *The Great Shoulder Drop.* When stress hits, your shoulders often try to make a break for your ears. Stop them in their tracks by taking a deep breath, shrugging your shoulders up as high as you can, holding for a few seconds, and then letting them drop like you're dramatically tossing a heavy backpack. Repeat a couple of times. It's surprisingly satisfying and way less weird than it sounds. Bonus: it also makes you look super chill, like you're shrugging off life's nonsense—literally.

If your jaw is feeling tighter than a jammed pickle jar lid, try *The Jaw Wiggle.* Open your mouth wide like you're about to devour the world's largest sandwich. Then, gently move your jaw from side to side. You might even feel or hear a little pop as things loosen up. If the idea of this exercise feels silly, just think about how much energy your jaw is wasting on clenching. Better to give it a wiggle and save that energy for eating actual sandwiches.

Next up is *The Pretend Stretch.* No time to hit the gym? No problem. Just stretch wherever you are, pretending like you're reaching for something that's juuust out of reach—an imaginary cookie, your goals, or maybe the life you planned before adulthood hit. Stretch your arms as high as they'll go, then tilt slightly to each side for a little extra length. This not only releases tension but also gives you a quick posture reset, so you look less like a question mark and more like an exclamation point.

For those glued to their desks, *The Seated Twist* is a lifesaver. Sit tall, place one hand on the back of your chair, and gently twist your upper body to one side. Hold for a few breaths, then switch to the other side. It's a mini detox for your spine, helping you wring out the stress like it's a stubborn dishcloth. Plus, it's subtle enough that your coworkers will just think you're super invested in swiveling for dramatic effect.

If you're feeling fidgety, try *The Finger Release.* Stretch your fingers wide, like you're trying to high-five the universe, then make a fist as tight as you can. Hold for a couple of seconds, and then release. Repeat this a few times. It's a great way to let go of stress that likes to hide in your hands (probably from all those emails you're typing). Bonus points if you do it while imagining you're crushing stress itself into oblivion.

Finally, there's *The Squeeze and Release.* Start at your toes, clench them tightly for a few seconds, and then let them go. Move up to your calves, thighs, and so on, working your way through your entire body until you've reached your face (yes, your face can clench, too). This progressive relaxation technique is like hitting the reset button on your muscles, and by the time you're done, you'll feel more like a human and less like a stress-stuffed scarecrow.

These physical relaxation exercises are easy, effective, and—let's be honest—a little fun. They're perfect for melting away tension without making a big production of it. The next time stress has you tied up in knots, try one of these quick fixes and remind your body that it deserves a little kindness, too. Who knew a wiggle or a twist could make such a difference?

Humor and Laughter as Instant Stress Relievers

If stress is the uninvited guest at your mental party, humor is the bouncer that can kick it out. Few things are as effective at lightening the load as a good laugh. Whether it's a quick chuckle, a full-on belly laugh, or one of those silent laughs where you look like a seal clapping for fish, laughter has magical stress-busting powers. And the best part? It's free, it's contagious, and there's no wrong way to do it.

Let's start with *The Comedy Quick Fix.* When stress hits, turn to something guaranteed to make you laugh—a funny YouTube clip, a goofy meme, or your favorite sitcom. Watching something light-hearted for just a few minutes can break the stress cycle faster than you can say "cat videos." Bonus points if you find something so funny that you accidentally snort. Not only does laughter release tension, but it also floods your brain with feel-good chemicals. It's like an emotional reset button disguised as entertainment.

Another great tool is *The Joke Swap*. Find a friend, coworker, or family member and exchange jokes—yes, even the groan-worthy dad jokes count. For example: "Why don't skeletons fight each other? They don't have the guts." (You're welcome.) Sharing a laugh not only helps you unwind but also strengthens your connection with the people around you. And honestly, is there anything more fun than trying to outdo each other with terrible puns?

For those who prefer a more physical approach, there's *The Fake Laugh Trick*. This one feels weird at first, but it works. Start by forcing a laugh—yes, even if you sound like an awkward villain in a B-movie. Keep it going for a few seconds, and before you know it, the fake laugh will turn into a real one. Why? Because your brain is easily fooled and starts releasing endorphins the moment it thinks you're having a good time. It's like tricking yourself into happiness, and who doesn't love a good life hack?

If you're feeling nostalgic, try *The Memory Giggle*. Think back to something funny that happened recently—a joke that caught you off guard, a silly mistake that made you laugh, or that time your pet did something absolutely ridiculous. Reliving these moments in your mind can spark fresh laughter and remind you that life isn't all stress and seriousness. It's a bit like re-watching your favorite comedy, except the star is your own life.

Another instant stress reliever is *The Laughter Chain Reaction*. Spend time with someone who has a contagious laugh. You know the type—once they start laughing, you can't help but join in, even if you have no idea what's funny. Laughter really is contagious, and being around someone who can't stop giggling is one of the fastest ways to catch the humor bug. Pro tip: kids are excellent for this— they'll laugh at the silliest things, and their joy is impossible to resist.

For those who want to take it up a notch, there's *The Laughter Yoga Experiment.* Yes, this is a real thing. It's a mix of breathing exercises and intentional laughter, and while it might sound a little strange, it's surprisingly effective. Imagine standing in a group, clapping your hands, and laughing for no reason—it's goofy, it's cathartic, and it works. Plus, the absurdity of the whole thing usually makes it even funnier, so you get double the laughs.

Laughter doesn't solve all your problems, but it does make them feel a lot less overwhelming. It's a reminder that even in stressful times, there's room for joy and silliness. So, the next time stress is weighing you down, find something to laugh about—it's like giving your brain a big, happy hug. And if all else fails, just remember: you survived this section of the book, so you're already winning.

How to Find "Mini-Stress Breaks" Throughout the Day

Stress loves to camp out in your brain like an annoying neighbor who doesn't know when to leave. But here's the good news: you don't have to wait for a vacation or a spa day to kick it out. Mini-stress breaks—tiny moments of calm sprinkled throughout your day—are your secret weapon. They're quick, easy, and surprisingly effective at keeping stress from taking over.

Let's start with *The Sip-and-Breathe.* Whether it's coffee, tea, or just water, turn your next drink into a mini-break. Take a sip, close your eyes (if you won't get weird looks), and take a deep breath. Focus on the warmth of the cup, the taste of the drink, or just the fact that you managed to hydrate today. This tiny moment of mindfulness gives your brain a much-needed pause, and let's be real—everything feels better with a beverage in hand.

Another favorite is *The Window Reset.* Got 30 seconds? Stand by a window, look outside, and just observe. Notice the trees swaying, the clouds drifting, or the chaos of the parking lot below. Let your mind wander for a moment without trying to "fix" anything. It's like a mental palate cleanser, and the change of scenery—even if it's just the neighbor's cat doing something questionable—is enough to give your brain a breather.

For a more active break, try *The One-Song Dance Party*. Put on your favorite song, crank up the volume (or use headphones if you're in a shared space), and dance like no one's watching—even if someone is. Dancing gets your blood flowing, shakes off tension, and is guaranteed to make you laugh at yourself at least once. Plus, it's hard to stay stressed when you're channeling your inner pop star.

If you're stuck at work, *The Desk Stretch* is a lifesaver. Roll your shoulders, stretch your neck, or stand up and touch your toes (or your knees—no judgment here). Even a quick stretch can release physical tension and make you feel like you're not entirely glued to your chair. Bonus points if you convince a coworker to join you for a spontaneous office yoga session.

Then there's *The Compliment Break*. Take a moment to think of something nice to say to yourself or someone else. Did you finally tackle that mountain of emails? "Great job, me!" Did your coworker bring snacks? "You're the hero we needed today!" Compliments are like mini mood boosters, and spreading a little kindness can lighten your own stress load while lifting someone else's day.

Lastly, try *The Gratitude Blink*. Close your eyes and think of one thing you're grateful for at that moment. Maybe it's your cozy sweater, the fact that lunch is only an hour away, or the simple joy of getting through a section of this book without needing a nap. Gratitude, even in its tiniest forms, can shift your perspective and make the day feel a little brighter.

The beauty of these mini-breaks is that they're quick, flexible, and don't require a lot of effort. They're like the fast food of self-care, except they're actually good for you. By sneaking these little moments into your day, you're giving yourself a fighting chance to stay calm and collected—even when life gets chaotic.

Now that you've got a toolkit for managing stress on the fly, it's time to look at a deeper layer of self-care: boundaries. In the next chapter, we'll explore how saying "no" and protecting your time isn't selfish— it's a form of self-care that can transform your daily life. Because let's face it, you can't pour from an empty cup—or take mini-breaks when everyone's asking for your attention.

ELEVEN

Creating Boundaries to Protect Your Self-Care Time

B oundaries are like the traffic cones of life—they're there to protect your space, but people will occasionally try to barrel right over them. Whether it's work emails after hours, family demands, or friends who think "no" is just a suggestion, creating boundaries is essential for protecting your self-care time. In this chapter, we'll explore how to set gentle yet firm limits that prioritize your well-being without the guilt. Because here's the truth: you can't take care of others if you're constantly running on empty.

Learning to Say "No" to Protect Your Time and Well-Being

For such a small word, "no" carries a lot of weight. It's like a magical spell that can instantly free up your time, preserve your energy, and protect your sanity. And yet, saying "no" often feels like navigating a minefield of guilt, obligation, and "what if they hate me now?" But here's the thing: every time you say "yes" to something you don't actually want to do, you're saying "no" to something you probably need—like rest, relaxation, or a minute to yourself. Learning to say "no" isn't just a skill; it's an act of self-care.

Let's start with *The Soft No.* This is perfect for those of us who hate conflict or worry about letting people down. A soft no sounds like, "I'd love to, but I can't right now," or "Thanks for thinking of me, but I have too much on my plate." It's polite, non-confrontational, and still gets the point across. The best part? Most people won't push back because, let's be honest, they've probably used the exact same line before.

Then there's *The Strategic No,* where you offer an alternative instead of outright declining. For example: "I can't make it this weekend, but how about next week?" or "I'm not available for that project, but I can help with something smaller." This approach shows you're still willing to contribute, just on your terms. It's like saying "no" with a side of "but here's what I *can* do," which is harder for anyone to argue with.

For those high-pressure moments when someone just won't take a hint, there's *The Firm No.* This is the equivalent of slamming down a drawbridge and guarding it with a dragon. A firm no doesn't require excuses, explanations, or apologies. It's a simple, "I'm not available for that," delivered with confidence and maybe a touch of mystery. The key here is to say it without overthinking. Remember: you don't owe anyone a reason for protecting your time.

One trick to make saying no easier is to blame your calendar. Try *The "Let Me Check My Schedule" Tactic.* When someone asks for your time, tell them you'll get back to them after checking your schedule. This buys you time to figure out if you actually want to say yes—or to craft the perfect no. If you decide it's a no, you can always say, "I checked, and unfortunately, I can't make it work right now." Voila! It's not you, it's your calendar.

Another lifesaver is *The "No Sandwich."* Start with something positive, deliver the no in the middle, and end on a kind note. For example: "I really appreciate you thinking of me. Unfortunately, I won't be able to join, but I hope it goes wonderfully!" This method is great for softening the blow while still standing your ground. Plus, it leaves the other person feeling appreciated, even if you declined their request.

Saying no is about prioritizing what matters most to you. If someone reacts poorly to your no, remember: that's their problem, not yours. Your self-care and well-being are worth more than any temporary discomfort you might feel about turning something down. Every time you say no to something that drains you, you're saying yes to yourself—and that's a win.

Setting boundaries starts with small, manageable steps. The more you practice saying no, the easier it becomes, and soon, you'll wonder why you ever felt guilty about it. After all, you deserve to protect your time and energy. And let's be real—who's going to take care of you if you don't?

Tips for Setting Gentle Boundaries at Work and Home

Setting boundaries at work and home can feel a bit like juggling flaming torches while riding a unicycle—it's intimidating, but with a little practice, you can master it without getting burned. The key is to set limits that are firm but kind, protecting your time and energy without alienating your coworkers, family, or roommates. It's all about the balance between standing your ground and keeping the peace.

Let's start with *Workplace Boundaries,* also known as "How to Protect Your Time Without Making Your Boss Hate You." One classic trick is *The Off-Hours Shield.* This involves setting clear boundaries for when you're available. For example, if your workday ends at 5 p.m., make it known that emails or calls after that time will be addressed the next day. You can even add a friendly note to your email signature: "I value my work-life balance and will respond during business hours. Thanks for understanding!" It's polite but gets the point across—your time is sacred after hours.

For those coworkers who think "urgent" applies to everything, try *The Polite Deflection*. When they pop by with a last-minute task, respond with something like, "I'd love to help, but I'm focused on a priority right now. Can we revisit this tomorrow?" This lets them know you're not ignoring them, but you're also not dropping everything for their request. And if you've got one of those colleagues who insists on oversharing their life story at your desk, there's always the subtle, "Sounds interesting—let's catch up later!" before turning back to your computer with purpose.

At home, *The Family Boundary Dance* often requires a little finesse. Kids, partners, and even pets can have an uncanny ability to sense when you're trying to carve out me-time. For this, try *The Visual Boundary*. When you're unavailable, use a clear signal—like closing a door, wearing noise-canceling headphones, or holding a book dramatically in front of your face. It's not foolproof (kids will always find a way), but it sends a strong message: "This is my moment. Proceed at your own risk."

For partners, *The Scheduled Check-In* is a game-changer. Set aside specific times to discuss things like plans, chores, or grocery lists instead of letting these conversations interrupt your relaxation time. For example, "Can we go over this after dinner? I'm taking a quick break right now." This approach keeps communication flowing but also protects your downtime. Bonus: It makes you look super organized, even if you're winging it.

If you're dealing with friends or extended family who don't respect your boundaries, try *The Friendly Firmness Approach*. For instance, if a friend keeps calling during your workout or meditation time, gently let them know: "Hey, I've started setting aside this time for myself, but I'd love to catch up afterward!" It's kind but makes it clear that your self-care comes first. And if Aunt Judy insists on dropping by unannounced, don't be afraid to say, "Next time, give me a heads-up so I can make sure I'm free!"

Finally, let's talk about *The Guilt-Free Boundary.* One of the hardest parts of setting boundaries is shaking off the guilt that comes with saying no or asking for space. But here's the truth: boundaries aren't about being selfish; they're about being sustainable. If you're constantly giving without recharging, you'll burn out faster than a cheap candle. Remind yourself that protecting your time and energy allows you to show up better for the people you care about.

Gentle boundaries are like invisible fences for your time—they keep you from being overwhelmed while still allowing for connection. By practicing clear communication, polite deflection, and guilt-free prioritization, you'll find it easier to protect your self-care time at work and home. And who knows? You might even inspire others to follow your lead.

How to Protect Your Recharge Time Without Feeling Guilty

Picture this: you've finally carved out a moment for yourself. You're sitting with a cup of tea, enjoying some peace and quiet, when the guilt monster sneaks in. "Shouldn't you be doing something productive?" it whispers. Sound familiar? Guilt has a way of showing up uninvited, especially when you're trying to recharge. But here's the thing: rest isn't a luxury—it's a necessity. And protecting your recharge time is one of the most selfless things you can do because a well-rested you is a better you.

Step one in guilt-free recharging is embracing *The Oxygen Mask Philosophy.* You've heard it before: on a plane, you're supposed to put your own oxygen mask on first before helping others. The same goes for self-care. If you're running on fumes, you're not much help to anyone. So, when you take time to recharge, remind yourself that you're not being lazy—you're refueling. A drained battery doesn't power anything, and the same goes for you.

Next up is *The Art of Scheduling Downtime.* Treat your recharge time like any other important appointment. Block it out on your calendar, set a reminder, and don't let anyone (including yourself) interrupt it. When someone asks for your time during your recharge block, you can politely say, "Sorry, I'm booked then." No one needs to know that your "meeting" is with your couch and a bowl of popcorn. The point is to protect that time as if it were sacred—because it is.

For those moments when guilt creeps in, try *The "Would I Judge Someone Else?" Test.* Imagine a friend told you they were taking an afternoon to rest because they'd been feeling overwhelmed. Would you call them lazy? Of course not. You'd probably applaud them for taking care of themselves. So why hold yourself to a harsher standard? Give yourself the same grace you'd offer a friend. If you wouldn't judge them for recharging, don't judge yourself either.

Sometimes, guilt comes from feeling like you're letting others down by stepping away. This is where *The Honest Heads-Up* comes in handy. If you're worried about people misunderstanding your need for downtime, communicate it clearly. For example: "I've been feeling a bit stretched thin, so I'm taking some time to recharge. I'll be back at it afterward." Most people will respect your honesty and appreciate that you're taking steps to avoid burnout. And if they don't? That's their issue, not yours.

Another guilt-busting strategy is *The Reframe.* Instead of seeing recharge time as "doing nothing," think of it as "investing in my well-being." Rest isn't a waste of time—it's what allows you to function. Athletes don't train 24/7; they rest and recover to perform their best. You're no different. Whether you're napping, meditating, or binge-watching your favorite show, you're giving your mind and body the care they need to keep going. That's not laziness; it's smart strategy.

Finally, don't underestimate the power of *The Quick, Effective No.* Sometimes, protecting your recharge time means saying no to things that don't serve you. If someone asks for a favor during your designated downtime, it's okay to say, "I can't right now, but let's connect later." Boundaries like this reinforce that your time is valuable, and you're not obligated to fill every moment with productivity or people-pleasing.

Guilt-free recharging takes practice, but it's worth it. By prioritizing rest and letting go of unnecessary guilt, you're showing yourself the respect you deserve. You're also setting an example for those around you—because if you can honor your need for downtime, maybe they'll start honoring theirs, too. And who knows? A well-rested you might just change the world—or at least your corner of it.

Strategies for Balancing "You Time" with Responsibilities

Ah, the eternal juggling act: balancing self-care with the endless parade of responsibilities life throws at you. It's like walking a tightrope while holding a dozen flaming torches—and someone keeps tossing you more. The good news? You don't have to choose between being a responsible adult and taking care of yourself. With a little creativity and planning, you can carve out "you time" without feeling like you've dropped the ball.

The first strategy is *The Time Audit.* Take a day or two to track where your time actually goes. You might discover surprising little pockets of opportunity, like the 10 minutes you spent scrolling social media or the 15 minutes you spent staring blankly at the fridge. These micro-moments are prime candidates for "you time." Instead of mindlessly losing them, reclaim them for something that recharges you—like reading a few pages of a book, stretching, or enjoying your coffee in peace.

Next up is *The Combo Move.* Sometimes, self-care and responsibilities can coexist. Folding laundry while listening to your favorite podcast? That's multitasking magic. Cooking dinner while belting out your favorite songs? Culinary self-care. By combining tasks with something that brings you joy, you're sneaking in self-care without adding extra time to your schedule. It's like turning chores into a stealthy recharge mission.

For the truly overbooked, there's *The Sacred Appointment Trick.* This involves scheduling "you time" into your calendar, just like you would a meeting or a dentist appointment. Whether it's 15 minutes of quiet in the morning, a quick walk at lunch, or a full hour on a weekend, treat this time as non-negotiable. When someone tries to book over it, confidently say, "Sorry, I'm busy then." The beauty of this approach is that no one has to know your "appointment" involves a bath bomb and a murder mystery novel.

If guilt about responsibilities creeps in, try *The Prioritization Filter.* Ask yourself: What truly needs to be done *right now,* and what can wait? Spoiler alert: most things can wait. Your email inbox will still be there in an hour, and the dishes aren't going to sprout legs and march away. By focusing on what's urgent and letting the rest sit for a bit, you create space for self-care without letting your to-do list take over your life.

Another helpful trick is *The Delegation Game.* Just because you can do something doesn't mean you should. Handing off tasks—whether it's asking your partner to take care of dinner or assigning chores to the kids—frees up time for yourself. And here's a pro tip: when someone says, "Just tell me how I can help," actually tell them. (Yes, they might regret asking, but that's their problem.) Sharing the load doesn't make you less capable; it makes you smart.

For those moments when responsibilities feel overwhelming, try *The Tiny Escape.* Even five minutes can make a difference. Step outside, close your eyes and take a few deep breaths. Or hide in the bathroom

—no judgment. These quick breaks might not seem like much, but they're like pressing the reset button on a stressed-out brain. Sometimes, "you time" is less about quantity and more about quality.

Finally, there's *The Imperfection Embrace.* Accept that you're not going to nail the balance every day—and that's okay. Some days, the laundry will pile up, emails will go unanswered, and your "you time" might be five stolen minutes in the car before you face the chaos inside. The important thing is that you're trying. Balance isn't about perfection; it's about doing your best with the time and energy you have.

Balancing "you time" with responsibilities takes effort, but it's worth it. By prioritizing self-care, multitasking smartly, and letting go of perfection, you're creating a life where both you and your responsibilities get the attention they deserve. And as we move forward, we'll dive into a chapter all about celebrating those wins—big and small—because you've earned it.

TWELVE

Celebrating Your Self-Care Wins (Big or Small)

S elf-care is one of those things we're all quietly crushing but never give ourselves credit for. You finally drank a full glass of water? Victory! Took a shower before you smelled like a middle-school gym sock? Absolute champion. This chapter is about throwing yourself the mini-parade you deserve. Life is hard enough without waiting for someone else to clap for you—so it's time to cheer yourself on, whether you just nailed a yoga pose or simply managed to not scream during rush hour traffic. No win is too small to celebrate, and yes, that includes putting on pants today.

Reflection Exercises to Acknowledge Your Progress and Efforts

When was the last time you gave yourself a genuine pat on the back? No, "not completely messing up" doesn't count as a celebration. Life moves fast, and we're all guilty of skipping the part where we acknowledge the good stuff we do—even the little wins that keep us sane. The truth is, reflecting on your self-care efforts isn't just a nice-to-have; it's essential for keeping the momentum going. And, spoiler alert: you've done more than you think.

Let's kick things off with *The "Look at Me Go" List*. Grab a piece of paper or open the notes app on your phone, and jot down everything you've done recently that counts as self-care. Did you take a nap? Write it down. Walked to the mailbox instead of driving? Add it to the list. Said "no" to a meeting that could've been an email? Double points. The goal here is to see, in black and white, just how much you're already doing for yourself—even if it doesn't feel like much. Because, guess what? It adds up.

If listing things out isn't your jam, try *The Daily Snapshot*. At the end of each day, think about one thing you did for yourself—just one. It doesn't have to be revolutionary. Maybe you drank water before coffee (an Olympic-level feat, let's be honest) or finally folded that laundry that's been mocking you for days. Reflecting on even the smallest effort creates a ripple effect, reminding you that self-care is an ongoing process, not an all-or-nothing event.

For those who like a little flair, there's *The Victory Jar*. Find an empty jar—or a bowl, or, hey, a shoebox if that's all you've got. Every time you do something that feels like a self-care win, write it on a slip of paper and toss it in. It can be as small as taking a deep breath when you were stressed or as big as finally scheduling that doctor's appointment. Over time, you'll have a jar full of evidence that you're absolutely nailing this self-care thing, even if it doesn't always feel like it.

Need something visual? *The Progress Collage* might be your speed. Print out photos of moments when you were taking care of yourself —your smiling face after a workout, that peaceful cup of tea, or even your triumphant grocery cart full of healthy snacks. Arrange them in a collage (physical or digital) that you can look at when you need a reminder of just how far you've come. Plus, who doesn't love an excuse to get crafty?

For the tech-savvy, there's *The Self-Care Log*. Download a habit-tracking app and start logging your wins. Brushed your teeth before noon? Logged. Ate something green? Logged. Took two minutes to stretch? Yep, that goes in too. Watching those small wins add up over time is like getting gold stars for being human—because let's face it, adulting deserves some sort of reward system.

Lastly, if you're more of a talker than a writer, try *The Mirror Pep Talk*. Stand in front of a mirror and tell yourself what you're proud of. Sure, it might feel a little silly at first, but hearing the words out loud has a way of sticking. Say something like, "You crushed it today by getting out of bed. Look at you go!" or "You didn't lose your mind in traffic—you're basically a Zen master." Over time, these mini pep talks become second nature, like having a tiny cheerleader in your head.

Reflecting on your self-care progress isn't about perfection—it's about celebrating the effort you're putting in, no matter how messy or small it feels. By taking a moment to acknowledge what you've done, you're reminding yourself that you're moving forward. And let's be real—sometimes, just surviving the day deserves a round of applause.

Creating a Self-Care Journal to Track What Works Best for You

Keeping track of your self-care efforts might sound like one more thing to add to your to-do list, but hear me out: a self-care journal isn't homework—it's your personal cheat sheet for figuring out what actually works for you. Think of it as a diary for your wins, your struggles, and all those "aha" moments when you realize that deep breathing actually does make you feel less like a frazzled squirrel.

First, let's talk setup. Don't worry; you don't need a fancy leather-bound journal or color-coordinated pens (unless that's your thing, in which case, go for it!). A basic notebook, a notes app, or even the back of a napkin will do the trick. The goal here isn't to create a masterpiece—it's to have a space where you can reflect on what's helping you feel human and what's, well, not.

Start with *The Daily Check-In*. At the end of each day, jot down three quick notes: what self-care activity you tried, how it made you feel, and whether it's worth repeating. For example: "Tried yoga. Felt like a pretzel but also kind of relaxed. Might give it another shot." Or, "Ate kale. No thanks. Not even if it's trendy." These small observations help you see patterns over time, like which practices make you feel amazing and which ones you're doing just to say you tried.

If you're not into daily entries, try *The Weekly Recap*. Once a week, take a few minutes to reflect on your self-care efforts. What worked? What didn't? Did you find a new favorite practice, or did you realize that bubble baths aren't actually your thing? (Pro tip: baths aren't mandatory for self-care—don't let Instagram convince you otherwise.) Summing it up weekly keeps things low-pressure while still giving you insights into your habits.

For a bit more structure, create *The Self-Care Grid*. Divide a page into categories like "Physical," "Mental," "Emotional," and "Fun," and list one or two activities under each. For instance, under "Physical," you might write "took a walk" or "didn't eat cake for breakfast (this time)." Under "Fun," maybe it's "watched a terrible rom-com and laughed at the plot holes." By spreading your self-care across categories, you're ensuring a more balanced approach—and also giving yourself permission to prioritize fun, which is 100% valid.

Feeling creative? Try *The Doodle Method*. Instead of writing everything out, draw little symbols or sketches to represent your self-care activities. A cup for drinking tea, a sun for getting outside, or a little heart for moments of gratitude. It's like turning your self-care journal into a visual diary that's way more fun to look back on.

Bonus: doodling itself can be a form of self-care, so you're basically doubling up.

One of the best parts of keeping a self-care journal is revisiting it when you're having a tough day. Flip back to see what's worked for you in the past—like that one time you danced around your kitchen and instantly felt better. It's a great reminder that you already have the tools to handle whatever life throws your way; sometimes, you just need to remember where you left them.

If the idea of a journal still feels daunting, think of it this way: it's not about perfection. It's about capturing little snippets of your self-care journey so you can figure out what makes you feel like your best self. No one's grading this thing (unless you want to give yourself gold stars, which, honestly, is kind of brilliant).

A self-care journal is your personalized guide to what works, what doesn't, and what makes you laugh along the way. It's a chance to celebrate your progress, learn from your experiments, and—most importantly—keep prioritizing yourself. Because let's face it: you're worth every page.

Tips for Celebrating Small Wins and Keeping Self-Care Fun

Self-care can sometimes feel like another box to check off, but here's a radical thought: what if it was actually fun? Celebrating small wins doesn't have to mean balloons and confetti (although, no judgment if you're into that). It's about finding simple, joyful ways to acknowledge your efforts and make the process of taking care of yourself something you actually look forward to.

Let's start with *The Mini-Reward System.* Treat yourself like the self-care rock star you are by setting up a reward system for your wins. Did you finally drink water before coffee this morning? That's a gold star moment. Literally—get some stickers and slap one on your calendar. Hit a bigger milestone, like finishing a workout program or actually flossing for a week straight? That calls for a treat, like a new book, a fancy coffee, or an evening dedicated to doing absolutely nothing. Rewards keep self-care from feeling like a chore and remind you that effort is worth celebrating.

Another fun idea is *The Victory Dance.* Every time you nail a self-care moment, celebrate with a goofy little dance. It doesn't have to be good (in fact, it's better if it's not). Channel your inner Elaine Benes or invent a new move called "The Floss Champion." Dancing releases feel-good endorphins and makes you laugh, turning even a small accomplishment into a party. Bonus: it's a mini workout, so you're technically doubling up on your self-care game.

For those who love visual reminders, try *The "I Did It" Jar.* Every time you do something that feels like a win—no matter how small— write it down and toss it in a jar. At the end of the week or month, read through your notes and marvel at how much you've done. It's like a time capsule of positivity, reminding you that you're constantly making progress, even if it doesn't always feel that way. Plus, it's satisfying to watch the jar fill up with proof that you're crushing it.

If you're more of a verbal person, there's *The Self-Care Shoutout.* Call or text a friend to share your win. Something like, "Guess who finally made it to the gym without immediately regretting it? This guy!" or "I said no to three things today and still had time to watch my favorite show." Celebrating out loud reinforces your effort, and if your friend joins in with their own wins, you've just started a self-care bragging club. Membership: two awesome humans.

For those who like to keep it light, try *The Silly Celebration.* Every time you hit a self-care milestone, do something ridiculous to mark the occasion. Maybe it's wearing a tiara while you fold laundry or eating ice cream with a tiny spoon like it's a royal dessert tasting. Adding humor to your celebrations keeps things fun and makes even the smallest moments feel special. Plus, it's hard to take life too seriously when you're wearing a crown.

Another tip is *The Theme Day Approach.* Dedicate a day to celebrating your self-care wins in style. Call it "Me-Tastic Monday" or "Self-Care Sunday," and spend the day acknowledging all the little things you've done for yourself recently. Treat yourself to your favorite meal, watch a feel-good movie, or take a guilt-free nap. It's like a holiday, except the only gift you need is a little time for yourself.

Finally, remember that self-care doesn't have to be perfect to be worth celebrating. Maybe your yoga session turned into five minutes of lying on the mat, or your "healthy dinner" was just a salad with extra croutons. That's okay! Celebrate the effort, not the outcome. The fact that you're trying is what matters, and that's always worth a little cheer.

By keeping self-care fun and celebrating your wins, you're making the process something to look forward to. So, throw yourself a mini party, laugh at the imperfect moments, and keep going—you're doing amazing.

Encouragement to Keep Experimenting with New Self-Care Ideas

Self-care isn't a one-size-fits-all deal. What works for one person might feel like torture to another (hello, kale smoothies). The beauty of self-care is that it's endlessly customizable—there's always a new idea to try, a fresh twist to add, or a hilariously bad experiment to laugh about later. This section is your official permission slip to get creative, try new things, and find what lights you up.

Let's start with *The "Why Not?" Method.* This involves asking yourself, "Why not try something different today?" Maybe you swap your usual walk for a dance workout, trade your cup of tea for a bright green matcha latte, or attempt a meditation app that promises to make you feel like a Zen monk. Even if it doesn't become a permanent addition to your routine, trying something new keeps self-care fresh—and gives you a story to tell. ("Did I love goat yoga? No. But was it memorable? Absolutely.")

For the adventurous, there's *The Bucket List Approach.* Write down a list of self-care activities you've always been curious about but never tried. Think big: pottery classes, forest bathing, joining a book club, or even making your own candles. Pick one item from the list and give it a go. Worst case? It's not your thing, and you cross it off. Best case? You discover a new passion. Either way, you're adding a little excitement to your routine, which is self-care in itself.

Another fun strategy is *The "What's Around Me?" Experiment.* Look at your surroundings and find inspiration. Got a dusty puzzle on a shelf? That's your next self-care project. A barely used waffle maker? Time for a breakfast extravaganza. Maybe there's a park you've driven by a hundred times but never visited. Exploring what's right in front of you is an easy way to shake things up without overthinking it. Plus, it's a reminder that self-care doesn't have to be complicated—it can be as simple as noticing what's already available.

If you prefer a low-commitment approach, try *The 5-Minute Test Drive.* Instead of diving headfirst into a new self-care activity, give it a quick trial run. Want to start journaling but hate the idea of writing pages every day? Set a timer for five minutes and jot down whatever comes to mind. Curious about yoga but afraid you'll topple over? Try one pose, laugh at yourself, and move on. The 5-Minute Test Drive takes the pressure off and lets you explore new ideas without feeling like you're signing a lifetime contract.

For those who love a little friendly competition, there's *The Self-Care Challenge.* Partner up with a friend and take turns picking a new self-care activity for both of you to try. Maybe they suggest a sound bath (whatever that is), and you counter with an art class. At the end of each challenge, compare notes. Did you love it? Hate it? Either way, you've shared a laugh and expanded your horizons—and probably learned more about what works for you.

If none of those ideas resonate, here's a wild concept: *Make Up Your Own Self-Care.* Who says self-care has to follow anyone else's rules? If baking pies at midnight feels restorative, do it. If standing in your driveway to look at the stars makes you happy, that counts. Self-care is personal, and the only "right" way to do it is the way that feels good to you. Embrace the weird, the wonderful, and the "wait, is this self-care?" moments.

The key to experimenting with self-care is staying open and curious. Not every idea will stick, and that's okay. What matters is that you're trying, exploring, and giving yourself permission to prioritize your well-being in whatever way works for you. So go ahead—try something new, laugh at the missteps, and celebrate the wins. You're officially the CEO of your self-care, and the possibilities are endless.

Conclusion

Congratulations—you made it to the end of this book, and guess what? That counts as self-care, too! Taking the time to reflect on your well-being, laugh at some ridiculous anecdotes, and pick up a few new ideas is no small feat. Self-care isn't about achieving perfection; it's about showing up for yourself in whatever way you can, day by day, moment by moment.

By now, you've learned that self-care doesn't require hours of meditating in a perfectly serene setting (though if you've got that, go for it). It can be as simple as pausing to breathe, finding humor in a chaotic moment, or saying "no" when you need to. Self-care isn't a chore—it's a habit of kindness toward yourself, one that grows stronger the more you practice it.

Let's be honest: life isn't going to slow down just because you've decided to prioritize self-care. Work deadlines will still loom, the laundry will still multiply like rabbits, and your inbox will still somehow fill up overnight. But now, you've got tools. You know how to carve out micro-moments of calm, protect your boundaries, and laugh at the inevitable self-care "fails" along the way. You've embraced the beauty of imperfection, celebrated your small wins, and maybe even created a mantra to carry with you. That's no small accomplishment.

The beauty of self-care is that it's never static. What works for you today might evolve tomorrow, and that's okay. Some days, self-care will look like a morning jog and a green smoothie. Other days, it'll look like staying in bed with a bag of chips and Netflix. Both are valid. Self-care isn't about doing what looks good on paper—it's about doing what feels right for you in the moment.

As you move forward, remember to celebrate every little effort you make. Drank some water? Amazing. Took a deep breath instead of losing your cool? Legendary. Managed to laugh when things went sideways? You deserve a trophy. These small moments of care add up, creating a foundation of resilience and joy that will carry you through even the busiest, most overwhelming days.

Most importantly, remember that self-care is a journey, not a destination. There's no finish line, no "perfect" routine, and no prize for being the most Zen person in the room (though if there were, you'd definitely be a contender). What matters is that you keep trying, keep experimenting, and keep showing up for yourself—because you're worth it.

As you close this book, take a moment to acknowledge the effort you've put into this journey. You've prioritized yourself, even if it was just for the time it took to read these pages. That's no small thing. Now, go forward with a little more kindness, a little more humor, and a whole lot of confidence that you've got this. After all, you're not just surviving—you're thriving, one small act of self-care at a time.

And if all else fails? Just remember: put on the tiara, eat the ice cream, and dance like nobody's watching because you've earned it.

A Helping Hand for Fellow Overwhelmed Humans

"Self-care isn't all bubble baths and face masks. Sometimes it's just muting a group chat." – Unknown

Hi there, self-care warrior! You've just finished *Self-Care(ish) Sanity Hacks*, where we tackled the chaos of everyday life, found humor in the overwhelm, and learned how to sneak self-care into even the busiest schedules.

Now, I have a favor to ask...

Would you be willing to help someone else on their self-care journey by sharing your thoughts about this book?

Imagine someone just like you—frazzled, busy, and barely hanging on to their sanity. They're juggling work, family, and endless to-do lists, desperately hoping to find small ways to breathe amidst the chaos.

Your review could be why they discovered this book the same way you did. It might give them the encouragement, the laugh, or the quick sanity-saving tip they didn't know they needed.

We have a simple mission: help as many busy, overwhelmed people as possible find peace, humor, and calm in their daily lives. Reviews help get the word out and make it easier for others to find this book when they need it most.

Could you leave a quick review on Amazon? It doesn't need to be long or perfect—just a few words about what made you smile, laugh, or breathe a little easier.

Your review could mean one more person realizes they're not alone in the chaos, one more reader learns how to find calm in the busiest of days, and one more family or individual embraces imperfect but meaningful self-care.

Scan the QR code below for a quick and easy way to share your thoughts.

Thank you for letting me be a part of your self-care journey. Your support, time, and kindness mean the world to me.

Here's to finding laughter and calm in the chaos—and sharing it with others.

With gratitude,

Avery Wells

9 7 9 8 3 4 8 1 0 9 2 3 3